Book Title:

ADHD: A Blessing or a Curse?
How to Transform the World's Most Misunderstood Brain Into a Precious Gift

Dedication & Acknowledgments

In Memory of:

My dear mother, **Tzila bat Davied** — *Sylvia L. van der Velde Duis* —
A woman of strength, faith, and unwavering belief in Hashem.
She was taken from this world at the age of 92.

In Honor of our beloved father, **Benno (Benyamin ze'ev ben Davied Zwi (Davied- hartog van der Velde)**, may he be well, they had the courage and foresight to save my life time and again.
Despite the unbearable weight of their own history—losing nearly their entire families in the horrors of World War II, and growing up without the steady presence of parents—they never gave up on me.
With deep patience and Hashem's help, they raised me, guided me, and believed in me when others did not.
I owe them everything.

In Honor

Of Chani Mizrachi Root, previously van der Velde my ex-wife mother of our children.
  Who, long before I understood ADHD, recognized that I was not a failure or a fool—only a soul with unchanneled energy and fire.
  She stood beside me when almost no one else did.
  She believed in my potential, helped me find ways to manage and direct my ADHD, and devoted herself to raising our children with love, strength, and resilience.
  In many ways, she raised them largely on her own, shaped them into the exceptional human beings they are today, and never wavered in her loyalty or her love.
  May she be blessed for all she gave, all she carried, and all she became.

© Copyright Page – ADHD: A Blessing or a Curse?

© 2025 Dovied Zwi van der Velde/ home safe home inc. the amazing people organization
All rights reserved.

No part of this publication may be reproduced, stored in a retrieval system, or transmitted in any form or by any means—electronic, mechanical, photocopying, recording, scanning, or otherwise—without prior written permission from the author, except in brief quotations used in reviews or scholarly discussion.

SECOND EDITION, 2025
Published by Dovied Zwi van der Velde - **Home Safe Home Books / Amazing People Press**
Email: **homesafehome613@gmail.com**

ISBN: 979-8-999765-0-0-0

Printed in the United States of America.

© **COPYRIGHT PAGE – ADHD: A Blessing or a Curse?**

For permissions, bulk orders, translations, and foreign rights inquiries, contact the publisher at the email above.

Cover design, interior layout, typography created by: Dovied van der Velde

All names, characters, and events presented as examples or case studies are either used with permission or are fictionalized to protect privacy.

Introduction

- **Why this book?** Understanding ADHD is more than just a scientific or medical exercise—it is a journey into what it means to be human. This book was born out of a desire to reframe ADHD from being seen as a limitation into a pathway to potential.
- **Who this is for:** This book serves parents, adults, educators, and leaders who want to navigate the challenges of ADHD with compassion and insight.
- **What this book is not:** It is not a pity party, nor is it merely a medical manual. It is a guide to transformation, not just for those with ADHD, but for everyone who loves, teaches, or works with them.
- **Besides, modern research, the basic knowledge of this book, is from living it, as an ADHDer myself, and having children who are ADD etc.** AND b"H all came out beautifully with wonderful lives and families, and everyone is a pillar in his or her community. Most importantly I AM SO PROUD OF YOU ALL!!!

The author.

Table of Contents

Chapter Outline	06
1: what is ADHD	09
2: The Hidden Gift unmasked potential	27
3: Chaos or Creativity – Rethinking the ADHD Mind	38
4: The Battle Within – Emotions, Impulses, and the ADHD Heart	49
5: The Classroom Struggle, Education	60
6: ADHD in Adulthood — Identity, Career, and Relationships	86
7: The Role of the Support System — No One Thrives Alone	100
8: What the World Gets Wrong About ADHD	114
9: Building a Personalized ADHD Strategy	131
10: Relationships, ADHD, and the Challenge of Connections	138
11: Relationships, ADHD, and the Challenge of Connection	149
12: Workplace Realities	159
13: ADHD in the Classroom	165
14: Medication, Supplements, and Natural Tools	175
15: Navigating Burnout, Overwhelm, and Shutdown	185
16 Love and Mariage with ADHD	194
ABOUT THE AUTHOR.	206

Chapters Outline:

Part I – Understanding the Struggle

1. What Is ADHD?

Clinical definitions (DSM-5)
Subtypes: inattentive, hyperactive-impulsive, combined
Neurological and brain chemistry factors
Misdiagnosis vs. underdiagnosis
ADD Through the Ages
Historical misunderstanding
Cultural attitudes (e.g., ADHD in America vs. Europe)
Famous "Addiers" from Mozart to Einstein to Simone Biles
Living with ADHD
Case studies: child, teen, adult, spouse
The rollercoaster of emotion and executive dysfunction
Shame, blame, and the loss of identity
The Jewish View & Other Religious Perspectives
ADHD and divine purpose
Midrashic insight into "different minds"
Other faith views on "difference" and soul gifts

Part II – The Gift Within
Hyperfocus and Creativity
Why some of the greatest minds had ADHD
The "ADD Advantage" in entrepreneurship, invention, and music
From Surviving to Thriving
Habits, structure, and coaching that turn chaos into creativity
Neuroplasticity and how ADHD brains can be rewired
Emotional resilience and spiritual perspective
The Role of Support Systems
Family dynamics
Teachers and schools
Employers and colleagues
Spouses and marriage

What the World Gets Wrong About ADHD
Myths debunked
Stigma and shame vs. empowerment and advocacy

Part III – The Way Forward
Faith, Focus, and Function
How faith-based tools help
Meditation, tefillah (prayer), and mindfulness
Torah vs. modern psychology – bridges and boundaries
Building a Personalized ADHD Strategy

Daily planner methods
Time-blocking for impulsive minds
Self-talk, journaling, and apps
Parenting an ADHD Child
Seeing beyond the "problem"
Creating structure and play
Disciplining with dignity
Love and Marriage with ADHD
When one or both partners have ADHD
Communication breakdown and breakthrough
How "Addiers" love differently — and more deeply

ADHD and the Soul's Mission
Rethinking the labels
What if ADHD is the spark we need?
Living unapologetically — yet with accountability

Appendices
ADHD vs. Autism: Distinctions and overlaps
Daily ADHD planner pages (templates)
List of support groups and organizations
Recommended readings, Torah sources, and secular research

CHAPTER 1

What Is ADHD?

The Misunderstood Brain That Can Change the World

"They said I was restless, noisy, disruptive.

They did not know I was listening to music the world had not written yet." Ludwich Von Beethoven.

I. The Label Before the Life

Imagine being trapped inside a brain that races like a Ferrari… with bicycle brakes. You see patterns others don't but miss the ones they expect. You feel everything, *always*. You want to behave, but you act before you think. You begin a sentence with a brilliant idea—and forget it halfway through.

This is not laziness. This is not lack of discipline. This is **Attention-Deficit/Hyperactivity Disorder**, or **ADHD**—a condition so misunderstood, so mislabeled, that its greatest victims often are not its symptoms, but the shame imposed by others.

ADHD is not a curse. Nor is it merely a blessing. It is a *power*. And like any power, it depends on how it is channeled.

II. The Clinical Picture

According to the **Diagnostic and Statistical Manual of Mental Disorders, Fifth Edition (DSM-5)**, ADHD is defined as:

"A persistent pattern of inattention and/or hyperactivity-impulsivity that interferes with functioning or development."

This condition must manifest in at least two settings (e.g., home and school or work) and must have been present before the age of 12. ADHD is diagnosed by clusters of symptoms that fall into two main categories:

1. Inattentive Type (ADD-like presentation)

- Often fails to give close attention to details
- Has difficulty sustaining attention
- Appears not to listen when spoken to directly
- Struggles to follow through on instructions

- Avoids tasks requiring sustained mental effort
- Loses things
- Easily distracted
- Forgetful in daily activities

2. Hyperactive-Impulsive Type

- Fidgets or squirms
- Leaves seat when expected to remain seated
- Runs or climbs in inappropriate situations
- Unable to play or engage in leisure activities quietly
- Talks excessively
- Blurts out answers
- Difficulty waiting turn
- Interrupts or intrudes on others

3. Combined Type

Both inattentive and hyperactive symptoms are present.

III. ADHD Is Not a Deficit

Ironically, the term "attention-deficit" is misleading. Individuals with ADHD do not have a *lack* of attention—they often have *too much* attention, distributed poorly. It is not a deficit of attention. It is a **regulation disorder**—of attention, emotion, and impulse.

ADHD is a challenge of *executive function*. Executive function is the brain's CEO—the part that organizes time, emotion, decision-making, and memory. In those with ADHD, the CEO shows up late, speaks softly, and takes frequent coffee breaks.

IV. How the ADHD Brain Works

Neuroscientific research using **fMRI** and **PET scans** has demonstrated that ADHD brains have:

- **Dysregulation in dopamine pathways**, especially in the prefrontal cortex and basal ganglia.

- **Delayed cortical maturation**, particularly in the frontal lobe.

- **Reduced activation in reward-processing regions**, which causes motivation to be external rather than internal.

Put plainly: the ADHD brain has trouble doing something unless it's:

- **New**
- **Urgent**
- **Interesting**
- **Immediately rewarding**

This explains why a child with ADHD can play video games for hours but will not do three minutes of math homework. It's not manipulation—it is **neurological architecture**.

V. The Emotional Fallout

Living with ADHD is more than dealing with disorganization or forgetfulness—it is living in a world that constantly punishes you for who you are.

Children with ADHD often:

- Are criticized more than praised

- Are disciplined more than understood
- Internalize the belief: *"I am bad,"* instead of *"I am struggling"*
- *Abuse of stimuli*

Adults with undiagnosed ADHD may:

- Bounce from job to job
- Experience failed relationships
- Struggle with self-worth and shame
- Be misdiagnosed with depression or anxiety
- Abuse of stimuli prescribed and non-prescribed.
- At times of excessive or hyper concentrations. Bordering or looking like Aspergers.

According to Dr. Edward Hallowell, psychiatrist, and author of *Driven to Distraction*:

"The real problem for people with ADHD is not that they are disordered. It is that they are misunderstood, under-supported, and never taught how their brains truly work."

VI. Famous Minds with ADHD

Would it surprise you to know that many of history's greatest thinkers, creators, and changemakers likely had ADHD?

Here is a sampling of names believed to have had it (by modern retrospective criteria, or openly diagnosed):

Wolfgang Amadeus Mozart

Composed music in his head at age 5, moved constantly, jumped between projects. Sound familiar?

Albert Einstein

Forgetful, spacey in class, daydreamed endlessly—but redefined science.

Thomas Edison

Expelled from school at age 12. Called "addled." Built the world's greatest invention laboratory.

Steve Jobs

Uncontrollable at Apple. Constantly shifting ideas. Obsessive about design. Changed how we live.

Jim Carrey

Open about his ADHD and use of humor to channel it. Once said, "My energy could either destroy me or make me rich."

Michael Phelps

ADHD diagnosis in childhood. His mother says swimming saved him from school failure. He won more Olympic medals than anyone in history.

These people were not broken. They were differently wired. They had trouble with conformity—but they redefined creativity.

VII. A Torah View: The Neshama That Will not Sit Still

Judaism has never shied away from struggle. We do not erase the faults of Avraham, Moshe, or David Hamelech. We embrace brokenness as a path to greatness.

There is a famous teaching:

"L'fum tzaara agra" – "According to the struggle is the reward" (Avot 5:23).

What if an ADHD child, who struggles ten times harder to focus in Tefillah, gets **ten times the reward** for trying?

What if Hashem created the ADHD soul not for punishment, but for *mission*?

The Rambam writes that every person has a unique derech, a unique mission. Some are slow and steady. Others are passionate, impulsive, bursting with energy. The Torah doesn't demand sameness—it demands **honesty**, **growth**, and **self-mastery**.

Moshe Rabbeinu had a speech impediment—but was chosen to speak to kings. Your ADHD is not what holds you back—it is what sets you apart.

VIII. A Day in the Life: The Unseen Struggle

Let us walk with Yaakov, a 9-year-old boy with ADHD.

7:30 AM: Yaakov wakes up, already running late. He is dressed but forgets his tzitzits. Breakfast is a blur—he spills cereal, loses his spoon, then laughs at something on the floor.

8:15 AM: In class, he stares out the window. His Rebbe calls his name—he did not hear the question. His classmates giggle. He feels stupid.

10:00 AM: Recess. Yaakov is a superstar—he is fast, funny, full of life. But then he accidentally bumps a boy too hard and gets sent inside.

12:00 PM: Lunch—he forgot his sandwich. Again.

2:00 PM: He finally finishes a worksheet. Smiling, he brings it up—only to realize he did the wrong side.

3:00 PM: On the bus home, he kicks his feet. He does not mean to bother anyone. But the driver yells again.

By bedtime, Yaakov is exhausted. Not from play. But from trying to be what the world wants him to be.

And still, the next morning, he tries again.

This boy is not a failure. He is a warrior.

IX. ADHD Is a Spectrum

It is important to understand that ADHD is not binary. It exists on a spectrum—from mild to severe—and affects people differently. Some:

- Function well with mild executive dysfunction

- Struggle socially but excel creatively
- Have co-existing conditions: anxiety, OCD, dyslexia, ASD, Tourette's

Each person's "ADD" is their own. Diagnosis is important—but understanding the person is even more so.

X. Girls with ADHD – The Silent Sufferers

ADHD in girls is often **missed because** it presents differently:

- Less hyperactivity, more internal distraction
- More compliant behavior
- Higher rates of daydreaming, perfectionism, social anxiety

As a result, many bright girls suffer silently diagnosed only after years of emotional damage. Studies show girls with undiagnosed ADHD have **higher rates of depression, self-harm, and eating disorders.**

They are not less affected—they are **less seen.**

XI. The Medication Debate

Stimulant medications (e.g., **Ritalin**, **Adderall**) are often prescribed for ADHD. These work by increasing dopamine and norepinephrine in the brain, enhancing attention and impulse control.

But medication is not magic. It:

- Works well for some
- Creates side effects for others
- Should never be the only treatment

ADHD management is a toolbox:

- Medication
- Coaching
- Behavioral therapy
- Exercise and nutrition
- Supportive environments
- Faith and meaning

The best treatment is *integrated*, not isolated.

XII. Beyond the Label: A Vision for the Book

This chapter has shown the complexity of ADHD. But this is just the beginning.

We will explore:

- How to unlock the hidden strengths of ADHD
- How to build tools that *fit* the ADHD mind
- How parents, teachers, and spouses can become partners—not punishers
- What a spiritual insight and practical strategy can build a thriving life

You are not here to be "fixed."

You are here to be *understood*. And then unleashed.

ADHD Through the Ages – From Shame to Superpower"

I. A Condition Without a Name

Throughout human history, there have always been individuals who did not quite "fit." The child who could not sit still. The adult who leaped into five projects but finished none. The one who always interrupted, or forgot, or felt things "too much." These people often lived without explanation—only labels: "difficult," "rebellious," "lazy," or worse.

What we now know as **Attention-Deficit/Hyperactivity Disorder** (ADHD) had no name in the ancient world, but its traits have always existed. The story of ADHD is a story of misunderstanding, of misdiagnosis, of silencing—and, eventually, of rediscovery and recognition.

This chapter explores how societies throughout history dealt with people whose brains worked differently—and how, in modern times, science, education, and even spirituality began to reframe ADHD not as a defect, but as a different dimension of human potential.

II. Ancient Minds, Modern Traits

Even in biblical and Talmudic times, we find mention of children who could not focus, who interrupted or were impulsive. Though the language of neuropsychology did not exist, our Sages addressed behavior, discipline, and development in great detail. The *Mishnah* and *Gemara* are filled with stories of students who struggled, questions about children's capacities, and debates over the proper way to teach a child "according to his way" (חנוך לנער על פי דרכו).

Was ADHD hiding in plain sight?

In ancient Greece, philosophers like Socrates and Plato wrote of students with "scattered" minds. Some Roman generals were noted for their bursts of energy and short tempers. In medieval Islamic and Jewish scholarship, there were mentions of children who were brilliant but "could not sit." None of these were considered medical problems—just parts of a person's character.

The lack of diagnosis meant many went unnoticed or misunderstood. Those who conformed to social norms were praised. Those who did not were disciplined—or discarded.

III. Early Modern Period – Morality vs. Medicine

As psychology developed in the 17th to 19th centuries, the Western world began to pathologize behavior that deviated from the "norm." A child who did not pay attention was seen not as different—but as disobedient. There was little concept of neurological diversity.

In the 1800s, medical papers began to appear describing "mental restlessness." In 1902, British pediatrician **Sir George Still** gave a series of lectures on children who were "incapable of moral control," despite being intelligent. He described what we now call ADHD—but framed it in terms of willpower and morality, not neurology.

This misunderstanding was disastrous for children. Schools punished them, parents blamed themselves, and many children internalized the idea that they were simply "bad."

IV. The 20th Century – A Name, But Not Yet Compassion

The term **hyperkinetic impulse disorder** appeared in the 1930s. Later came terms like "minimal brain dysfunction." None of these labels offered dignity—they often intensified stigma.

During the 1950s and 60s, stimulants like **Benzedrine** and later **Ritalin** were introduced to help children who could not focus. But the diagnosis was often reactive used only when a child became "too difficult" in class. And the treatment? Often just medication, without emotional or educational support.

ADHD remained misunderstood. It was associated with boys who could not sit still. Girls who daydreamed quietly were overlooked. Adults were not even considered.

In some communities—particularly religious or traditional ones—ADHD was not spoken of at all. Spiritual failure was blamed instead of neurological difference. A boy who could not sit through *davening* was seen as irreverent. A girl who forgot her obligations was seen as careless. No one asked: *What if this is how Hashem made them?*

V. The 1980s–1990s: The Shift Begins

The revolution began when scientists started using brain scans (like PET and MRI) to show real differences in the ADHD brain. Regions involved in attention, impulse control, and reward response showed distinctive patterns.

Researchers began to speak of **executive dysfunction**, not just "bad behavior." Educators learned that ADHD was not a failure of effort—but of **regulation. Advocates**, too, began to rise—parents, doctors, and even public figures speaking openly about their experiences. The idea of **neurodiversity** gained traction: that brains come in different types, and each offers unique strengths.

But while the science progressed, the **stigma remained**. Many teachers still called these children "lazy." Many communities still hid the diagnosis out of shame.

Chapter 2: The Hidden Gift – Unmasking the Potential Within

The diagnosis of attention deficit hyperactivity disorder (ADHD) often arrives as a thunderclap—an uninvited label that seems to split a child's future into two. On one side: misunderstanding, impatience, disappointment, and stigma. On the other: a lifetime of managing a "disorder." But what if we challenged this split perception? What if, hidden behind the restlessness, distractibility, and impulsivity, there lies an untouched well of brilliance and potential?

This chapter invites you to walk through a different door—not into a clinic, but into the soul of the ADHD mind. Here, we won't ask, "What is wrong with this child?" but rather, "What is trying to emerge from this mind that we haven't yet learned to hear?"

From Deficit to Difference

Let us start with the language itself. "Attention Deficit Hyperactivity Disorder." It implies a lack of attention, excess energy, and dysfunction. But any parent, teacher, or friend who has sat long enough with a child or adult with ADHD knows this is not a deficit of attention—it's an overflow. It is the inability to **filter** attention. It is not that they cannot focus. It is that they **cannot stop focusing** on everything at once.

The late Dr. Edward Hallowell, a Harvard-trained psychiatrist, and an ADHD expert himself, famously said:

"ADHD is not a disorder of not paying attention, it's a disorder of **too much attention**—to everything."

This reframing is not just semantic. It is critical. A deficit suggests damage. A difference suggests diversity. And in the right context, diversity is a strength.

The Evolutionary View

Let us zoom back in time. Imagine a tribe of early humans navigating the savannahs of Africa. Most of the tribe are methodical, steady, and predictable. But then there is that one person—always alert, jumping at every sound, easily bored, a risk-taker, noticing every change in the wind or shadow in the trees.

That person had ADHD. And that person highly likely **saved the tribe**.

In evolutionary psychology, it is proposed that ADHD traits were advantageous in hunting, gathering, and detecting danger. Impulsivity could mean faster decision-making in crisis. Hyperactivity was stamina on the move. Distractibility meant higher sensitivity to environmental shifts.

Today, in classrooms or offices, these same traits are framed as impairments. But the mind has not changed—the context has.

Seeing the Forest and the Trees

Individuals with ADHD often see connections others do not. Their associative brains jump tracks quickly, often arriving at unique or surprising conclusions. This is not disorganized thinking—it is **non-linear** and **pattern-seeking** thinking.

Imagine a child drawing a picture. While most children draw a house with a sun, the ADHD child draws a universe filled with planets, comic book heroes, and lines that do not make sense—until suddenly they do. The child has drawn not a picture, but a story. One that unfolds in all directions at once.

This is not random. This is the forest and the trees, all at once. It is not a curse. It is raw, unfiltered perception.

The Struggle Is Real – And So Is the Strength

None of this is to deny the challenges ADHD brings. Children with ADHD may struggle academically, socially, and emotionally. Adults may face chronic lateness, impulsive decisions, failed relationships, and frustration.

But the mistake is assuming that the struggle is the whole story.

In fact, the same qualities that lead to difficulty in structured environments are often the exact ones that lead to brilliance in unstructured, creative, or high-stimulation environments. The hyperfocus of ADHD—yes, **hyperfocus**—can lead someone to spend 14 hours straight designing a video game engine, composing a symphony, or learning every nuance of aviation history.

Yes, ADHD can bring suffering—but it can also bring **sublime intensity**.

Meet the Addies

Let us pause to meet our heroes: the *Addies*. This is not a clinical term—it is a nickname, an endearing badge for those living with ADHD. The Addie is the child who races down the hallway, humming ideas, forgetting his backpack but inventing a new way to tie shoelaces. The Addie is the teen who cannot sit through math class but rewrites the school play in a single night. The Addie is the adult who loses track of time but has built three businesses by the age of 30.

They are not broken. They are wired differently. And we must stop confusing difference with deficiency.

The Role of Education and Systems

Why, then, do so many Addies fall through the cracks?

Because the systems we place them in were built **against** their nature.

Most school systems reward conformity, stillness, linear learning, and timed responses. But the ADHD mind thrives in **movement, exploration, challenge, creativity**, and **meaning**. A mind that asks "Why?" and "What if?" is rarely satisfied by "Because I said so."

This is not to blame teachers. It is to challenge the **structure**.

Children with ADHD are often told to sit still when they learn better moving, to focus on one task when their strength is in integrating many, to follow a rigid routine when their minds crave rhythm, not rigidity.

We need schools that reward divergent thinking, allow movement, incorporate art, and story, and offer flexible pacing. In short, we need schools that **adapt to the mind**, not the other way around.

The Jewish Lens – A People of Unboxed Thinkers

Let us bring in a Torah lens, if briefly.

Moshe Rabbeinu, our greatest leader, had speech difficulties. Yitzchak Avinu preferred the quiet indoors, while Yaakov was an intense learner and Eisav a man of the field. Yosef dreamed in riddles. David HaMelech danced before the Aron, weeping in song, a whirlwind of spirit and battle.

The Torah is full of Addies.

In Chassidus and Kabbalah, we are taught that every soul has a unique light. The ADHD soul may be one whose light does not sit neatly in vessels—it overflows. But that overflow is its beauty. As the Zohar says, **"There is a breaking of vessels so the light can spread."**

Famous Addies Who Changed the World

Still skeptical?

Let's look at a few known or likely Addies:

- **Albert Einstein** – Disliked school, daydreamed often, failed early verbal tests.

- **Thomas Edison** – Couldn't sit still, was labeled as "slow."

- **Walt Disney** – Fired from a job for "lacking imagination."

- **Leonardo da Vinci** – Couldn't finish a painting without starting ten others.

- **Simone Biles** – Olympian with ADHD.

- **Michael Phelps** – Swimmer with ADHD who won 23 Olympic gold medals.

- **Mozart** – Known for hyperactive, impulsive, and eccentric behavior.

- **Will Smith** – Publicly discussed his ADHD.

- **Solomon Schechter** and **Rav Avraham Yitzchak HaCohen Kook** – deep thinkers whose writings suggest creative minds that flowed faster than the page could catch.

These are not people with deficits. They are people whose **gifted minds could not be boxed**.

Harnessing the Power

So what do we do with all this?

We **reframe. Rebuild. Rekindle.**

1. **Reframe**: We stop viewing ADHD as a defect. We begin seeing it as a **difference**—one that brings unique challenges, yes, but also **superpowers**.

2. **Rebuild**: We build systems that **accommodate** and **nurture** divergent minds. Flexible education, creative workspaces, mentorship-based therapy.

3. **Rekindle**: We reignite the **self-esteem** of the Addies. So many have been told they are lazy, bad, unteachable. We must become their mirrors, reflecting back their light.

A Word to the Parents

If you are reading this with the heavy heart of a parent trying to do their best—know this:

Your child is not broken.

They may not fit the mold. But maybe the mold is the problem.

Your child may need a different approach—more movement, fewer lectures, more compassion, fewer punishments, more curiosity, and fewer comparisons.

Try asking:

- "What helps you feel calm?"
- "What makes you feel smart?"
- "What's the hardest part of your day?"

Your job is not to fix them. Your job is to guide them to **discover themselves**. With love, patience, and partnership.

A Word to the Teachers

You are not powerless.

Even one adult who "gets" a child with ADHD can change their entire life trajectory. Research shows that **one trusted adult** is enough to buffer the negative outcomes of ADHD. Be that adult.

Give space for curiosity. Allow movement breaks. Offer choices. Teach with visuals. Connect, then correct.

And most of all—**see their soul**, not just their report card.

A Word to the Addies Themselves

Yes, you.

If you've ever been told you're too much, too loud, too fast, too intense—here's what I want to say:

You are **not too much**. You are exactly enough.

The world was not built for minds like yours—but that doesn't mean you don't belong. It means the world needs to change.

Your mind is a river—wild, rushing, unpredictable—but also nourishing, beautiful, and deep.

You may have to work harder to build your bridges. But once you do, you can cross into places others can't even imagine.

The "Curse" Is Real—but So Is the "Blessing"

This book is not about sugarcoating the real pain ADHD can bring. Marriages suffer. Jobs are lost. Fines pile up. Children cry themselves to sleep.

But it is also true that the very fire that burns us can also light the world.

The pain is real. So is the power.

The answer lies in not rejecting the fire—but **learning to become its master**.

Transforming the Label

Imagine if, instead of ADHD being seen as a red flag, it became a **signal**—a signal that a unique kind of brain is at work. A brain that may need support, yes, but also one that may carry answers, ideas, and talents the world desperately needs.

Let us stop pathologizing difference. Let us begin celebrating it.

Let us stop trying to "normalize" Addies—and instead, empower them to **normalize themselves**.

Conclusion: The Fire Within

There is a Hebrew phrase, "Chanoch l'na'ar al pi darko" – "Educate the child according to his way." Not the school's way. Not the system's way. **His** way.

Because when you honor the path of an Addie, you don't just improve outcomes—you save lives. And perhaps, just perhaps, you unleash the fire that will light up the world.

Chapter 3: Chaos or Creativity – Rethinking the ADHD Mind

Step into the mind of a person with ADHD. Now, try to stay there for one minute.
You'll see thoughts zigzagging through corridors, bouncing off walls, and colliding with memories, song lyrics, what-if questions, existential doubts, and forgotten errands. You'll hear a symphony that shifts from crescendo to stillness in seconds. You'll feel an electric current, a persistent hum of "what now?" and "what next?" and "what if?"

To most neurotypical observers, this inner world may feel like chaos. But to the person living inside it, it is a vibrant, unfiltered canvas. The problem isn't the storm—it's that no one ever taught them how to steer the ship within it.

This chapter explores one of the most misunderstood paradoxes of ADHD: that what looks like chaos from the outside may, in fact, be a form of creativity—potentially one of the highest forms of it. If we dare to look again, not with clinical detachment but with curiosity and compassion, we may uncover the real treasure within what many label as disorder.

Creativity: Not a Side Effect, But a Core Feature

In common narratives, creativity is treated as a "side benefit" of ADHD. Something accidental. "Well, yes, he's scattered, but he's very imaginative." But this thinking misses the point. Creativity is not a lucky accident in ADHD—it is often the very essence of how the ADHD brain is wired.

Creativity, defined broadly, is the ability to connect unrelated ideas, to think divergently, to take mental risks, and to imagine something that isn't there. These are not *exceptions* in ADHD—they are the rule.

Psychological studies confirm this. In one notable paper published in the *Journal of Creative Behavior*, researchers found that individuals with ADHD scored higher in originality and idea generation than their neurotypical peers. They produced more ideas, and their ideas were less conventional.

The reason? Their minds are less bound by filters. They don't discard the "irrelevant" as quickly, and so they stumble upon connections others miss.

The ADHD Brain: Wired for Divergent Thinking

Let's go deeper. Neuroimaging studies show that individuals with ADHD often have differences in brain connectivity—particularly in the default mode network (DMN), which is active during rest, daydreaming, or imagination.

In many people with ADHD, this network is "always on"—even during tasks. That means their minds drift naturally toward expansive, associative, creative processing.

To a teacher, this looks like zoning out. To a neurologist, it's hyperactive DMN activity. To an artist? It's the birthplace of genius.

The ADHD brain is not designed for linear, step-by-step problem solving. It thrives in **associative landscapes**. It's the mind that sees how music theory relates to math, or how the color of the sky changes the emotional tone of a sentence. It doesn't follow logic—it leaps to meaning.

But What About the Mess?

Ah, the clutter. The missed deadlines. The piles of unfinished work. Isn't that proof that ADHD is dysfunction?

Not quite.

The reality is more subtle. ADHD doesn't *prevent* task completion—it just doesn't naturally prioritize in the same way. Tasks that feel artificial, boring, or imposed are often rejected by the brain's reward system. But tasks that feel urgent, exciting, or meaningful get turbocharged attention.

This is why someone with ADHD can forget to pay rent but spend six hours researching the mating rituals of arctic foxes. Not because they're irresponsible—but because one task triggers dopamine, and the other doesn't.

Many artists, writers, inventors, and entrepreneurs with ADHD learn to live with a degree of "mess." Their desks are chaotic, their folders overflowing, their calendars patched together. But their *ideas* are crisp, vibrant, and often years ahead of their time.

The Myth of Discipline

A painful myth surrounds ADHD: the belief that if someone would just "try harder," they would be fine. But ADHD is not a character flaw. It is a neurodevelopmental difference that affects executive functioning—planning, inhibition, time awareness, and impulse control.

What looks like laziness is often overwhelm. What looks like apathy is often burnout. What looks like rebellion is often shame.

No one wants to fail. But when your mind doesn't follow the maps others do, and when you're punished for that difference repeatedly, eventually you stop trying to read the map.

You start to believe you're defective.
And nothing kills creativity faster than self-contempt.

The Role of Flow and Hyperfocus

While ADHD is often associated with distractibility, it also has an extraordinary counterpart: **hyperfocus.**

Hyperfocus is the state where time disappears, attention sharpens like a laser, and the person becomes utterly immersed in the task. Contrary to myth, ADHD is not a constant lack of focus—it's an inability to regulate where focus goes.

For the ADHD mind, entering flow isn't a luxury—it's a necessity. It's the only state where their mind feels "quiet." It's the moment the noise recedes, and clarity arises. Hyperfocus can be dangerous when misdirected (e.g., hours lost in video games), but when guided toward art, code, invention, music, writing—it becomes **a superpower.**

The goal, then, is not to extinguish hyperfocus, but to **harness it.**

Disorder or difference?

Let's pause on a critical question: is ADHD a disorder, or simply a difference?

In some cases, the answer is clearly: both.

When ADHD leads to repeated failure, social isolation, financial ruin, and inner despair—it is undeniably a disorder in functional terms. But if the environment is adjusted, and the person learns tools, context, and support, that same brain may thrive.

The DSM—the psychiatric manual—defines ADHD by its impairments. But it doesn't define it by its **possibilities**.

Imagine if instead of diagnosing based only on what's missing, we also asked: "Where is the energy trying to go?"

That's the creative lens. It asks not "what is wrong?" but "what wants to emerge?"

Learning From the Artists

History is filled with creators whose lives bear all the hallmarks of ADHD:

Vincent van Gogh – explosive emotionality, deep immersion in art, erratic habits.

- **Emily Dickinson** – unconventional attention, intense focus on specific themes, nontraditional rhythms.//
- **Mark Twain** – unpredictable lifestyle, financial chaos, constant invention.
- **John Lennon** – boundary-pushing, provocative, hyper-creative, scattered yet visionary.

These weren't stable, color-inside-the-lines people. They were storm-riders. And their art was the surfboard.

We must remember creativity is not born in neat, sterile spaces. It is born in contradiction, in disorder, in the ache of misfit souls trying to say something that hasn't been said before.

When the World Says "No"

One of the most heartbreaking parts of ADHD is internalized rejection. So many Addies grow up hearing:

- "Why can't you just focus?"
- "Stop being so dramatic."

- "You always start but never finish."
- "You're so lazy."
- "You're too much."

Over time, these become scripts that run inside the mind. And the tragedy is, they drown out the very inner voice that leads to innovation.

But every person with ADHD who has made peace with themselves has had to go through a transformation. They've had to unlearn the lie that they are broken and relearn the truth that they are **uncontainable**.

Strategies for Cultivating Creativity in ADHD

This is not a book of quick fixes—but real strategies can help. Here are some keyways to turn chaos into creativity:

1. **Externalize Organization**: ADHD minds forget what they don't see. Visual calendars, whiteboards, color-coded cues, or sticky notes help keep creative minds on track.

2. **Use Timers and Sprints**: Set 25-minute bursts of work (Pomodoro Technique) with 5-minute

breaks. It helps channel attention in manageable doses.

3. **Create "Creative Safe Zones"**: Environments free of judgment, where expression can flourish without being evaluated.

4. **Work With Mentors, Not Managers**: Creative ADHD minds need guidance, not micromanagement. A mentor nurtures, asks, listens, and believes.

5. **Celebrate Progress, Not Just Completion**: Many projects will remain half-finished. That's okay. Celebrate what *was* created, not what wasn't.

6. **Treat the Body, Nourish the Brain**: Sleep, movement, omega-3s, and mindfulness all enhance attention and mood regulation.

7. **Honor Intensity**: Don't punish the passion. Channel it.

A Word to Schools

If schools want to nurture creativity, they must allow it to be messy.

The ADHD child may not submit neat papers or follow the essay structure, but they might invent a story that moves an entire class. They may blurt out thoughts, but those thoughts may crack open a conversation. They may doodle instead of listening, but they are **processing** in ways we don't always recognize.

To educate an ADHD child is to **partner with the storm**—not to stop it, but to help it dance.

The Spiritual Side of Chaos

In Jewish thought, there's a deep awareness of the creative power of chaos. In the opening verses of Genesis, the world begins as "tohu vavohu"—formless and void. From that primal chaos, creation begins.

In Kabbalah, this is echoed in the concept of **"Shevirat HaKelim"**—the breaking of vessels, allowing divine light to scatter and reform in new patterns. Chaos is not destruction—it is **the prelude to creation**.

ADHD may be a form of modern tohu—a soul bursting with light, seeking vessels strong enough to hold it.

From Survival to Mastery

The journey of a person with ADHD is often marked by survival—getting through school, avoiding shame, learning to mask. But the real victory comes not in surviving ADHD, but in **mastering it**.

Mastery doesn't mean perfection. It means **ownership**.

- Knowing what works and what doesn't.
- Knowing when to say yes—and when to say no.
- Knowing how to protect your spark from the winds of criticism.

It means stepping into your life as the creator—not the casualty—of your story.

Closing Thoughts: The Revolution Starts Here

We have reached a turning point in how the world sees neurodivergence. No longer do we speak only of deficits and disorders. We speak now of **profiles**, **patterns**, and **potential. The** ADHD revolution will not be standardized. It will not be quiet. It will not wait in line. It will be sung, danced, coded, painted, filmed, and shouted. It will be lived in bold color, even when the world demands beige. The Addie soul does not want permission—it seeks **purpose**. And when purpose meets passion, chaos transforms into creation.

4: The Battle Within – Emotions, Impulses, and the ADHD Heart

At the heart of every person with ADHD, there is a battlefield.

Not a war between good and evil, but a constant tug-of-war between thoughts and feelings, impulses and logic, hope and shame. It is a silent battle fought in classrooms and kitchens, boardrooms and bedrooms, and often no one else even knows it's happening. Because on the outside, the person may appear cheerful, distracted, impulsive, or energetic—but inside, a storm is brewing.

If Chapters 1 through 3 explored the brain and creativity of ADHD, this chapter turns inward—into the emotional core. Because ADHD is not just about focus. It is about **feeling**. It is about **intensity**. And it is often about **pain**.

But it is also about deep empathy, passion, sensitivity, and resilience. The ADHD heart, though misunderstood, is one of the richest and most vibrant hearts a person can have.

Let's explore the emotional journey of the ADHD mind—not just its struggles, but its hidden depths and strengths.

The Emotionally Charged Brain

Neuroscientists have discovered that individuals with ADHD have structural and functional differences not only in the prefrontal cortex (which governs executive function), but also in areas of the brain responsible for emotional regulation—such as the amygdala and limbic system.

This means that people with ADHD don't just feel emotion. **They feel it more quickly, more intensely, and often for longer** than their neurotypical peers.

One small criticism can feel like a dagger. One compliment can light up their day for hours. One moment of rejection can haunt them for weeks.

This isn't weakness. It's **neurological sensitivity**. It's living without emotional filters. And while that can be overwhelming, it also makes for a uniquely emotionally intelligent individual—when given the right support.

Rejection Sensitivity Dysphoria (RSD)

One of the most common but least understood traits in people with ADHD is something known as **Rejection Sensitivity Dysphoria** (RSD). This is an extreme emotional reaction to the perception—real or imagined—of rejection, criticism, or disapproval.

A teacher says, "Please try to stay on task," and the student hears, "You're a failure."
A friend cancels plans, and the person hears, "You're not worth my time."
A romantic partner is quiet, and the person hears, "You're about to be abandoned."

This response is not a choice—it is a **surge** of emotional pain, often felt physically. People with ADHD may hide these reactions to avoid seeming "too sensitive," but internally, the suffering can be enormous.

This is why so many individuals with ADHD become **people pleasers**, perfectionists, or avoidant. They'd rather not try than risk being rejected.

The ADHD Shame Spiral

At the intersection of impulsivity, forgetfulness, and social awkwardness lies the greatest emotional danger: **shame**.

A person with ADHD often finds themselves saying the wrong thing, interrupting at the wrong time, forgetting the important task, or reacting too strongly. These moments, repeated over time, create a painful narrative:

"Something is wrong with me."
"I always mess up."
"Everyone else gets it—I don't."

This shame doesn't just linger—it **grows**.
It becomes a second skin.
And worst of all, it silences the very voice the world needs to hear.

Because when you're drowning in shame, you stop sharing, stop risking, stop dreaming. You become your own critic, harder on yourself than anyone else could be.

Impulsivity: The Emotional Accelerator

Impulsivity in ADHD is often misunderstood as just "doing without thinking." But at its core, impulsivity is emotional. It is the inability to pause between **feeling** and **acting**.

Someone cuts you off in traffic—you scream. You feel hurt—you send a long, intense message. You're bored—you spend money impulsively.

These actions aren't rooted in malice or immaturity. They're rooted in **neurological urgency**—the feeling that something must be expressed, or the pressure will explode.

This is why many ADHD individuals also struggle with mood swings, anger bursts, or over-apologizing. Their emotional brakes are weaker, not because they don't care—but because the brain doesn't always give them time to **slow down**.

The Gift of Emotional Depth

And yet—there's a flip side. A glorious one.

The same emotional intensity that brings struggle can also bring **extraordinary empathy, compassion, passion, and love**.

People with ADHD often notice the unspoken, feel the room, intuit others' emotions. They can be fiercely loyal, deeply caring, and emotionally intuitive in ways that surprise even therapists.

They're the ones who cry during commercials, who get angry at injustice, who feel joy with their whole being. When they love, they love **completely**.

This is the ADHD emotional gift. Not fragility, but **depth**.

The challenge is to learn how to live with that depth, without being consumed by it.

Emotional Regulation Strategies

There is no "off switch" for feelings—but there are **tools** that help manage them more skillfully. These include:

1. **Pause Practices** – Teaching the brain to wait before reacting. This can include deep breaths, counting to ten, or using phrases like "Is this helpful?"

2. **Naming Emotions** – "Name it to tame it." Teaching kids and adults to say: "I feel rejected" instead of acting out the pain.

3. **Reframing Thoughts** – Challenging the internal critic: "They didn't answer my message" becomes "They're probably busy—not rejecting me."

4. **Self-Soothing Rituals** – Music, movement, weighted blankets, prayer, art—these are not luxuries but lifelines for emotional grounding.

5. **Therapeutic Support** – Coaching, therapy (especially CBT or DBT), and support groups can help retrain emotional responses and provide community.

6. **Body-Based Regulation** – The body stores emotions. Yoga, dance, even a walk can reduce emotional overload.

7. **The Role of Trauma**

ADHD does not always come alone. Many people with ADHD also carry **complex trauma**, especially from childhood.

Why?

Because when you are constantly told you're wrong, bad, lazy, disruptive—or simply "too much"—it becomes internalized. The world, in trying to fix you, may accidentally **wound you**.

And for neurodivergent children, the trauma is often not one big event—but **thousands of little ones**. The sigh of a teacher. The eyeroll of a parent. The laughter of classmates. The endless corrections. The detentions. The labeling.

Trauma wires the brain for survival. And if you grow up constantly in survival mode, you can't grow emotionally, because your energy is spent protecting yourself.

Healing ADHD isn't just about focus. It's about **repairing the wounds of misunderstanding**.

The Spiritual Heart of the ADHD Journey

From a Jewish perspective, every soul is created with a unique light and mission.

Some souls are born to build, some to lead, some to heal—and some to **feel deeply and awaken others**.

The ADHD soul is one whose light is often too bright for standard vessels. It spills, spills, spills—overflows the limits of schedules, boxes, rules. But that same light, once held with compassion, can **illuminate the world**.

Our sages teach that the heart is the seat of wisdom. The Torah warns us not to follow the heart blindly ("לא תתורו אחרי לבבכם"), but also tells us to serve God בכל לבבך—with *all* our heart, including its chaotic parts.

The journey of the ADHD heart is to go from **reaction to response**, from **impulse to insight**, from **emotional confusion to emotional truth**.

Family Dynamics and Emotional Echoes

ADHD rarely exists in a vacuum. It affects families deeply.

Parents may feel frustration, guilt, exhaustion, or helplessness. Siblings may feel overlooked or jealous. And spouses may feel confused, especially when their partner seems inconsistent loving one moment, distant the next.

It's essential to recognize that many emotional clashes in ADHD families stem not from bad intentions, but from **misaligned emotional tempos**.

For example:

- The ADHD child needs time to decompress, but the parent needs structure.
- The ADHD spouse wants spontaneous connection, while the other craves predictability.

Without awareness, these mismatches create **shame cycles**: one person feels misunderstood, the other feels hurt, and both retreat emotionally.

The solution is emotional literacy, compassion, and clear communication.

The Power of Apology and Repair

No one is perfect. And in ADHD families, emotional outbursts, forgotten promises, or miscommunications are common.

But the most powerful tool any family can use is **repair**.

Learning to say:

- "I'm sorry I yelled."

- "I was overwhelmed and didn't handle it well."
- "I love you, even when I get frustrated."

These moments of vulnerability **rebuild trust**.

And when modeled consistently, they teach children (and adults) that emotions aren't dangerous—they are **opportunities for connection**.

Embracing Emotional Intensity as a Strength

In a world that often demands emotional neutrality, people with ADHD offer a gift: **emotional intensity**.

This intensity, though challenging, is also what fuels:

- Activism
- Art
- Innovation
- Spiritual yearning
- Deep relationships

The goal is not to flatten this emotional range, but to **refine it**. To teach the person with ADHD that their feelings are **valid but** not always **guiding lights**.

That they can *feel deeply* and still *act wisely*.

That they can *burn with passion* and still *choose kindness*.

Conclusion: The Heart Is the Compass

If ADHD is a journey, the brain is the map—but the **heart is the compass**.

And though that heart may beat faster, stronger, and sometimes erratically, it beats with **authenticity**. It seeks truth. It craves love. It longs for purpose.

The work of the ADHD soul is not to silence that heart, but to **befriend it.**
To listen to its pain. To honor its joy.
And to learn, with time, how to use that emotional fire not to burn—but to warm the world.

Because behind every distracted glance, every impulsive act, every emotional storm—there is a heart that **wants to love and be loved**, fiercely.

That is not a disorder.
That is the **beginning of redemption**.

Chapter 5 The Classroom

ADHD, Education and the Search for Belonging

Introduction

Classrooms are designed to reward sustained attention, orderly behavior and the ability to work within a set of unwritten social rules. For children and adolescents with **attention-deficit/hyperactivity disorder (ADHD)**, these expectations collide with neurological realities. ADHD is a neurodevelopmental disorder characterized by persistent patterns of inattention, hyperactivity and impulsivity. In 2022 a national U.S. survey estimated that **about 7 million children (11.4 % of those aged 3–17 years)** had ever been diagnosed with ADHD. Symptoms vary in severity—roughly six in ten children are classified as having moderate or severe ADHD and many live with co-occurring conditions such as anxiety or learning disorders. When these students enter school, rigid schedules and heavy emphasis on sustained concentration often exacerbate their difficulties.

This chapter explores how ADHD shapes students' experiences in the classroom. Drawing on recent research and guidance from educators, it examines the *academic*, *social* and *emotional* challenges they face and highlights interventions that foster a sense of belonging and success.

Academic obstacles

Distractibility, hyperactivity and executive dysfunction

At school, ADHD symptoms manifest in ways that undermine academic performance. Adolescents with ADHD often struggle to maintain focus, organize assignments and complete tasks on time. **Inattention** makes it hard to listen to instructions or follow multi-step tasks, while **executive functioning deficits** impair planning and time management. Hyperactivity and impulsivity may lead to constant fidgeting or blurting out answers, which can disrupt both the student and peers. As one teacher with ADHD notes, fidgeting helps students generate dopamine and maintain focus; banning fidget toys can therefore deprive them of an effective self-regulation tool. Allowing discreet movement (e.g., distributing worksheets or short stretching breaks) can harness hyperactivity productively.

Another often-misunderstood feature is **hyper-focus**—an intense, laser-like concentration on a preferred topic. People with ADHD do not lack attention; they struggle to control it. Minimizing distractions and weaving students' special interests into lessons can boost engagement.

Organizational training and behavioral management

Evidence-based classroom interventions can help. **Behavioral classroom management** uses reward systems or daily report cards to encourage positive behaviors and discourage negative ones. The Centers for Disease Control and Prevention (CDC) reports that this teacher-led approach increases academic engagement and works across age groups. **Organizational training** teaches time-management, planning and organization skills and has been tested with children and adolescents. Despite their effectiveness, only about one-third of children with ADHD receive behavioral classroom management.

Students who meet certain eligibility criteria may receive accommodations through an **Individualized Education Program (IEP)** or a **504 Plan**. IEPs provide specialized instruction and services under the Individuals with Disabilities Education Act (IDEA), while 504 Plans offer changes to the learning environment under the Rehabilitation Act. Accommodations can include extra time on tests, tailored assignments, positive feedback, use of assistive technology, scheduled breaks, and environmental modifications. Collaboration among teachers, parents and healthcare providers is essential;

most children with ADHD are not in special education but still need daily assistance.

Social challenges and the search for belonging

Difficulty interpreting social cues

ADHD affects not just academics but also *social interactions*. Executive-function impairments hinder turn-taking, waiting and self-monitoring, which are critical for conversation. Children with ADHD may interrupt, talk excessively or miss social cues The Foothills Academy notes that they can become bored, distracted or overwhelmed during interactions; peers may interpret this as disinterest or rudeness, leading to avoidance. A lack of successful social experiences creates a negative cycle in which children avoid future interactions, and their confidence erodes Because peer relationships teach cooperation, perspective-taking and conflict resolution, social isolation can impede emotional development and academic collaboration.

Rejection-sensitive dysphoria and emotion regulation

Many individuals with ADHD experience **rejection-sensitive dysphoria (RSD)**—intense emotional pain triggered by perceived rejection or failure.

An episode can produce rage, anxiety and plummeting self-worth. Simple classroom practices, such as allowing students to select their own teams, can accidentally trigger RSD when a child is left unchosen,. Educators can mitigate these risks by assigning teams or using random name generators and by teaching emotional literacy to all students.

Emotion regulation difficulties in ADHD stem from a hyper-responsive "fight-or-flight" system Students may react strongly to perceived injustice Teachers can help by clearly explaining rules, avoiding public reprimands, and ensuring consistent fairness.

Executive dysfunction and school culture

Up to 90 % of children and adolescents with ADHD struggle with **executive dysfunction**, which affects organization and time management Symptoms such as forgetting homework, untidy appearance and poor time keeping are often misinterpreted as laziness Quietly offering support and reducing embarrassment can preserve students' dignity and prevent defiance Strict uniform or appearance policies may disproportionately penalize students whose morning routines are already overwhelming

The importance of belonging in an inclusive classroom

Why belonging matters

Feeling valued and included in school influences wellbeing and academic success. The Learner Variability Project defines **belongingness** as feeling personally valued, included and supported by others. Students who perceive a strong sense of belonging report greater happiness, self-efficacy and academic motivation, Conversely, students with ADHD are at risk of isolation: difficulties with self-regulation may be viewed as behavior problems, and they often struggle to understand the hidden curriculum—the unspoken social rules of classroom. Teacher support is one of the strongest predictors of a learner's sense of belonging; when students feel respected, valued and treated fairly, they are more likely to engage.

Fostering belonging through inclusive practices

Inclusive classrooms deliberately create environments where neurodiverse learners feel safe and valued. Strategies include:

Key inclusive strategies	Evidence or rationale
Positive teacher–student relationships	Teacher support predicts a strong sense of belonging; students need to feel respected and treated fairly. Teaching Learning Lab+1
Culturally responsive and neuro-affirming teaching	Recognizing students' varied backgrounds and learning styles validates their identities and reduces feelings of marginalization. PubMed+1
Behavioral and organizational interventions	Reward systems and organizational training improve academic engagement and reduce disruptive behavior. PMC+1
Accommodation (IEP/504)	Providing extra time, breaks, tailored assignments and reduced distractions helps students manage ADHD symptoms. PMC
Clear communication and structure	Instructions thatent feedback, providing warnings before transitions and ensuring

Key inclusive strategies	Evidence or rationale
	instructions are understood prevents confusion.
Movement and sensory tools	Allowing fidget toys and short breaks harnesses hyperactivity and can enhance attention.
Assigning rather than choosing teams	Avoids rejection-sensitive triggers and fosters inclusive participation.
Role playing and social skills practice	Practicing turn-taking and perspective-taking at home or in class builds social competence.

Key inclusive classroom strategies for supporting students with ADHD
Evidence or rationale supporting each approach

Beyond the classroom: partnerships and advocacy

School success for students with ADHD relies on partnerships among educators, families and healthcare providers. Parents are often children's strongest advocates; they should familiarize themselves with their legal rights, such as IDEA and Section 504, and work with schools to secure appropriate services. Daily communication between teachers and parents—such as through a behavior chart—can reinforce positive behavior.

Healthcare providers can help families navigate medication and therapy options, while community programs offer social skills training and peer support. Ultimately, a holistic approach that considers academic accommodations, social-emotional support and family involvement is most effective.

Conclusion

ADHD reshapes the classroom experience. Students grapple with inattention, hyperactivity and impulsivity that make it difficult to meet conventional academic demands. These challenges spill into social interactions, leading to peer rejection, rejection-sensitive dysphoria and feelings of exclusion. Yet research and lived experience show that supportive environments can transform outcomes. Behavioral management and organizational training are evidence-based strategiescdc.gov. Inclusive practices that validate neurodiversity, provide accommodations and emphasize positive teacher–student relationships foster a sense of belonging source lvp.digitalpromiseglobal.org. When students with ADHD feel valued and understood, they are more likely to engage, succeed and thrive.

Walk into almost any traditional classroom, and you'll find neatly aligned desks, a teacher at the front, a board with instructions, and students expected to sit still, listen quietly, raise their hands, and follow the schedule.

Now imagine placing a child with ADHD in that room.

This child is intelligent, curious, energetic, and observant — but also restless, distracted, emotionally reactive, and often overwhelmed by structure. They fidget in their seat. They blurt out ideas. They forget their homework. They get praised one day and scolded the next.
And slowly, they begin to believe that school is not for them.
Worse — they begin to believe that they are **the problem**.

This chapter explores one of the most misunderstood arenas of ADHD: **education**.
It is here that many of the deepest wounds — and greatest misunderstandings — begin. But it is also here that redemption can begin, with awareness, adaptation, and compassion.

When the System Doesn't Fit the Brain

The modern classroom is largely designed for **neurotypical learners** — those who can:

- Sit still for long periods
- Focus on teacher-led instruction
- Follow sequential, linear learning
- Respond predictably to praise or correction

But children with ADHD do not fit neatly into these boxes. Their brains are wired for **movement, stimulation, curiosity, creativity, and novelty**.

They learn best when:

- They can move freely
- The material is relevant and exciting
- There's variety and flexibility
- Their emotions are engaged

In a traditional system, these needs are often not only unmet — they're viewed as problems to be corrected.

But what if, instead of asking "How do we fix the child?" — we asked, "How do we change the environment?"

Executive Dysfunction and the Hidden Barriers

A central challenge for students with ADHD is something called **executive dysfunction**.

Executive functions are mental skills that include:

- Working memory
- Organization
- Task initiation
- Planning and prioritization
- Emotional regulation

In school settings, these skills are crucial. They're the difference between finishing a project on time and forgetting it entirely, between taking notes and getting lost mid-sentence.

But a child with ADHD is not **choosing** to be disorganized or forgetful — their brain has real difficulty **accessing and coordinating** these systems under pressure.

Punishing them doesn't work. Shaming them is counterproductive.
What works is **scaffolding** — breaking tasks into steps, offering visual aids, and creating support structures.

The Impact of Labels

"You're lazy."
"You're disruptive."
"You're not trying hard enough."
"Maybe if you cared more…"

These are the wounds that many ADHD children carry from school.

Even if not spoken aloud, the **tone**, the **eyes**, the **body language** communicates volumes. Children absorb messages quickly — not just through feedback, but through the expectations that are **projected** onto them.

Eventually, the label becomes a self-fulfilling prophecy.

If a child hears "you're disorganized" enough times, they stop trying to organize. If they're called "the bad kid," they may as well **become** it — at least then they're in control of the story.

This is why **belief in the child** is not optional — it is essential.
The teacher who sees potential — despite the mess, despite the blurting out, despite the lost assignments — is the one who **changes lives**.

The Role of Movement and Sensory Input

Many children with ADHD need movement in order to think.

This is not metaphorical. Research shows that physical activity increases dopamine and norepinephrine in the brain — the very neurotransmitters that are **deficient** in ADHD brains.

This means:

- A child who paces while reading may actually **comprehend better**.

- A student who fidgets may be **regulating their alertness**, not just being annoying.

- A learner who doodles might be **organizing their thoughts** in images rather than words.

When schools demand stillness and silence, they may inadvertently **cut off access** to the child's natural learning mechanisms.

The solution isn't chaos. It's **structured flexibility** — allowing movement breaks, using standing desks, offering tools like fidget bands or balance chairs, and incorporating **kinesthetic learning**.

Homework and the After-School Meltdown

Parents of children with ADHD often face the same nightly battle:
Tears, resistance, anger, shutdown — all over **homework**.

Why?

Because after a full day of trying to "hold it together," the child is **exhausted** — mentally and emotionally. They've used up their energy on:

- Sitting still
- Inhibiting impulses
- Navigating social tension
- Managing frustration
- Processing verbal instructions

By the time they get home, they're in **cognitive and emotional depletion**.

The solution isn't more structure at home — it's **more understanding**, paired with adaptive support.

Examples:

- Break homework into small chunks

- Use timers with breaks
- Offer choices ("Which do you want to do first?")
- Praise effort, not outcome
- Consider reduced homework loads with school approval

When Intelligence Is Misunderstood

One of the greatest tragedies of ADHD in education is that **many of the brightest students are labeled as underachievers**.

Why?

Because school often rewards:

- Compliance over creativity
- Consistency over brilliance
- Memory over insight
- Neatness over novelty

The ADHD child may struggle with rote memorization, timed tests, or repetitive drills — but may be able to:

- Invent complex systems

- Solve real-world problems intuitively
- Engage in deep philosophical questioning
- Tell vivid stories and create rich metaphors

We must stop confusing **conformity with intelligence**.

Einstein famously said:

"Everybody is a genius. But if you judge a fish by its ability to climb a tree, it will live its whole life believing it is stupid."

The Teacher Who Changes Everything

Most adults with ADHD can tell you the name of the **one teacher** who believed in them.

It wasn't necessarily the most fun or lenient teacher — it was the one who **saw them**.

- Who let them stand while reading
- Who gave them leadership roles
- Who told them they were smart
- Who didn't mock them when they forgot their pencil

- Who encouraged their creativity

- Who gave them another chance

One adult who **truly sees** a child with ADHD can alter the course of that child's life.

Teachers don't just teach subjects — they **shape identities**.

Educational Alternatives and Innovations

Around the world, educators are exploring **alternative models** of learning that better serve children with ADHD:

- **Montessori Schools** – Emphasize hands-on learning, choice, and self-paced progress

- **Waldorf Education** – Integrates movement, arts, and emotional development

- **Project-Based Learning** – Focuses on creativity, teamwork, and real-life application

- **Forest Schools** – Outdoor learning that incorporates nature, play, and exploration

- **Home Education** – Customized pacing, curriculum, and emotional environment

- **THE EINSELGANGER EDUCATIONAL COMUNITY DESIGNED BY THIS WRITTER.** That hopefully we will be able to address in an separate book.

These models don't "cure" ADHD — but they often **stop pathologizing it**.
They work with the child's wiring instead of trying to overwrite it.

In conventional settings, accommodations like:

- Extra time on tests
- Oral presentations instead of written reports
- Alternative seating
- Visual aids and checklists
- Executive function coaching

— can make a dramatic difference.

The Emotional Cost of Academic Failure

For many children with ADHD, school is not a place of learning — it is a place of **failure**.

They see their peers succeed easily while they struggle.
They feel different — and often ashamed of that difference.
They are constantly corrected, redirected, reprimanded.

Over time, this leads to:

- Anxiety
- School avoidance
- Depression
- Behavior issues
- Negative identity development

The academic struggle becomes a **spiritual wound**. They stop seeing themselves as "learners" — and start seeing themselves as "failures."

Our job is not just to educate the brain — but to **heal the relationship between the child and learning**.

Parents as Advocates

Parents of children with ADHD must become **warriors** — not just caregivers.

They need to:

- Understand their child's learning style
- Request appropriate accommodations
- Meet with teachers and administrators
- Provide consistent support at home
- Educate themselves about ADHD
- Celebrate effort, not just grades

And most of all — they must remind the child:

"You are not broken. You are different. And your difference matters."

Advocacy is exhausting. But it is sacred work. Because when a child feels seen, protected, and championed — they begin to believe in themselves.

The Role of Torah and Jewish Thought

In Jewish tradition, **education is sacred**.

The word "chinuch" (חינוך) doesn't mean "teaching facts" — it means **initiating a soul into its path**.
As it says in Mishlei:

"חנוך לנער על פי דרכו" – "Educate the child according to his way."

Not *our* way. **His** way.

Our sages recognized that different children have different natures.
Some are quick. Some are reflective. Some are stormy. Some are serene.
The role of a parent and teacher is to uncover the **essence** of the child and guide them accordingly.

The ADHD child is not a mistake. He is a **challenge** — and a **gift**.
A divine soul with a fast-moving, high-voltage brain.
A spark that can light up the world — if we give it the right container.

The Chazon Ish is a major Torah authority of the 20th century. Modern psychological/medical categories ADHD did *not* exist in his language or era. Yet he had a lovely opinion which would fit so much into todays

ADHD teaching Chazon Ish on Educating Brilliant and Sensitive Children this is what he wrote:

You Cannot Break a Child's Nature he emphasized that chinuch (education) is to guide, not to break a child's nature.

Forcing uniformity damages a child's confidence and spiritual growth.

Brilliant Children Often Appear Unfocused He described children whose minds move faster than the classroom. Their restlessness often indicates high intelligence.

Forcing Such a Child Causes Harm Strict pressure crushes their inner spark. These children must not be forced into molds that do not match their nature.

These Children Need Warmth and Understanding He taught that sensitive and energetic children require patience, personal connection, and tasks suited to their strengths.

The School and the Teacher Must Fit the Child An educator who cannot understand a unique child should not "fix" him. Education must be individualized.

These Children Often Become Great Adults, scollars, and community leaders however if pressured wrong could go off.

Their intensity, creativity, and sensitivity—if protected—become sources of greatness.

Misbehavior Is Often a Sign of a Powerful Soul, looking for negative attention, since they stand out!

The Chazon Ish wrote that children who cannot sit still often possess rare spiritual strengths needing proper guidance.

- **Sources**

- Chazon Ish, Igros (Letters), Volumes I–III – guidance on children's natures and
- individualized chinuch.
- Chazon Ish, Emunah u'Bitachon – sections on character development and sensitivity of the soul.
- Oral traditions from students of the Chazon Ish (Rav Chaim Kanievsky, Rav Yaakov Yisrael
- Kanievsky).
- Chazon Ish's writings on chinuch as preserved in sefarim on his hanhagos and educational

Conclusion: Rewriting the Educational Script

The classroom can be a place of trauma — or a place of transformation.

It depends on:

- The teacher
- The parent
- The system
- And most of all — the **belief** we hold about the child

We must stop trying to make ADHD students "fit" into boxes.
Instead, we must **redesign the box**.

And in doing so, we don't just help those students — we create schools and systems that are more human, more creative, and more responsive for everyone.

The child who couldn't sit still may one day become the innovator who doesn't settle.

The girl who blurted out in class may grow into the woman who speaks truth no one else will voice. The teen who doodled through science may become the artist who inspires millions.

ADHD in the classroom is not a failure of attention. It is a call to pay **better attention** — to the learner, to the soul, to the spark. Let's listen.

Chapter 6: ADHD in Adulthood — Navigating Identity, Career, and Relationships

"I thought I'd grow out of it."
"I didn't know until I was forty."
"I always felt like I was faking being an adult."

These are the voices of adults living with ADHD — some recently diagnosed, some struggling in silence for decades. For many, ADHD isn't a childhood phase that magically vanishes after high school. It is a **lifelong neurological condition** with constantly shifting presentations and challenges.

In this chapter, we explore the journey of ADHD **after childhood**:
how it evolves, how it hides, how it disrupts — and how, with the right awareness and tools, it can be transformed into a source of **wisdom, innovation, and strength**.

The Myth of Outgrowing ADHD

One of the most persistent myths about ADHD is that it disappears with age.
This is both true and not true.

It's true that many children with ADHD learn **coping strategies** over time.
Their impulsivity may decrease. Their hyperactivity may

settle.
They may become better at **masking** their challenges.

But the core neurological profile — differences in executive function, attention regulation, dopamine pathways — **remains**.

In fact, for many adults, the **challenges become more invisible, but more impactful**:

- Missed deadlines at work
- Chronic lateness
- Disorganization at home
- Difficulty maintaining relationships
- Inconsistent follow-through
- Financial instability

ADHD in adulthood is often **less about physical restlessness** and more about **mental chaos**.

The internal soundtrack plays on:
"You're lazy."
"You're too much."
"You're not dependable."
And worst of all: "You're not enough."

How Adult ADHD Manifests Differently

While children with ADHD may be described as "hyper," "rowdy," or "spacey,"
adults often hear labels like:

- Disorganized
- Unreliable
- Inconsiderate
- Selfish
- Irresponsible
- Scatterbrained

That's because the world expects adults to "have it together."
When we forget a meeting, it's not cute — it's seen as careless.
When we interrupt someone, it's not playful — it's rude.
When we change careers or hobbies too often, it's called flakiness — not exploration.

But these surface behaviors often mask **underlying battles**:

- Difficulty prioritizing when everything feels urgent
- Paralysis when faced with open-ended tasks

- Overwhelm at the smallest administrative chore

- Emotional dysregulation triggered by shame or failure

ADHD adults aren't immature. They're **carrying invisible weights** through a world not designed for their wiring.

Diagnosis Delayed: The Silent Epidemic

For decades, ADHD was considered a "boy's problem." Girls were overlooked. Quiet dreamers were ignored. And when those children grew up, they became **undiagnosed adults** — millions of them.

It's estimated that **only 20% of adults with ADHD are diagnosed**.

That means the majority:

- Struggle without understanding why

- Internalize blame

- Are misdiagnosed with depression, anxiety, or personality disorders

- Receive inappropriate treatment

- Never gain access to the tools that could liberate them

For some, the diagnosis comes after their child is evaluated.
They see themselves in the symptom list — and everything clicks.

The moment of diagnosis is often bittersweet:

"I wasn't broken. I was just wired differently."
"All those years I was trying to be 'normal' — and beating myself up for failing."
"I finally understand who I am."

The Workplace Battleground

ADHD adults often struggle in traditional job settings.

The demands of modern work — multitasking, email overload, paperwork, team meetings — are tailored to the neurotypical brain.

For someone with ADHD, this can lead to:

- Starting projects with enthusiasm, but not finishing
- Struggling with time management

- Forgetting appointments
- Missing details
- Avoiding tasks that feel boring or overwhelming
- Conflict with authority due to impulsive communication

Ironically, ADHD adults can also be **brilliant, driven, and creative**.
They think outside the box.
They spot patterns others miss.
They thrive under pressure — when they care.

But success is inconsistent.
One day they're a genius, the next day they can't send an email.

This inconsistency creates shame — and shame triggers paralysis.
It's a vicious cycle.

Accommodations can help tremendously:

- Flexible hours
- Standing desks
- Delegation of admin tasks
- Verbal instead of written communication

- Clear deadlines with reminders

Entrepreneurship is also common — many ADHD adults prefer to create their own rhythm rather than fit into someone else's.

But without support or structure, even a passion project can become a source of **overwhelm and collapse**.

ADHD and Emotional Intensity

Adults with ADHD don't just struggle with focus — they often feel **everything more deeply**.

This is called **emotional dysregulation**, and it shows up as:

- Intense reactions to small events
- Difficulty recovering from criticism
- Sudden mood shifts
- Rejection-sensitive dysphoria (RSD)

RSD is a phenomenon where perceived criticism — even subtle or imagined — causes **intense emotional pain**. It feels like a physical wound.

That's why ADHD adults may:

- Avoid relationships
- Over-apologize
- Become defensive quickly
- People-please
- Quit jobs or friendships suddenly

The emotional landscape of ADHD is often filled with storms — quick to rise, slow to settle.

But this same sensitivity is also a source of **compassion, intuition, and creativity** — if it's understood and supported.

Relationships and ADHD: When the Wiring Collides

Love is challenging enough.
Add ADHD into the mix — and it becomes a dance of misunderstanding, frustration, and sometimes, magic.

Common struggles in ADHD relationships:

- Forgetting anniversaries, plans, or agreements
- Zoning out during conversations

- Interrupting often
- Emotional outbursts
- Difficulty with chores or parenting consistency
- Unequal division of mental labor

For the non-ADHD partner, it may feel like:

- "I'm doing everything."
- "You don't listen."
- "You don't care enough to try."

But the ADHD partner may feel:

- "I'm failing you."
- "I'm trying harder than you know."
- "I don't know why I can't just get it right."

With support, therapy, and mutual compassion, relationships can **thrive**.

Some tools:

- External reminders (shared calendars, alarms)
- Weekly check-ins

- Clear, non-accusatory communication
- Appreciation for effort, not just results
- ADHD education for both partners

Love with ADHD requires patience — but also yields **depth, passion, and playfulness**.

The Financial Toll

ADHD doesn't just affect emotions — it often hits the wallet.

Symptoms like impulsivity, forgetfulness, and disorganization can lead to:

- Missed bills
- Overdrafts
- Credit card debt
- Forgotten subscriptions
- Lost paperwork
- Failed budgeting attempts

Many ADHD adults live with **financial shame**, feeling incompetent or irresponsible.

But when we look closer, we often find **a lack of skill-building**, not a lack of willpower.

Solutions include:

- Automating finances
- Using visual budgeting apps
- Working with ADHD coaches
- Breaking tasks into tiny steps
- Building reward systems for small wins

With the right system, even ADHD minds can become **financially empowered**.

Spirituality and the ADHD Soul

Many adults with ADHD describe a **deep inner life** — a constant stream of thoughts, questions, and yearnings.

They often ask:

- "What's my purpose?"
- "Why am I like this?"
- "Where do I find peace?"

Traditional spirituality can sometimes feel rigid. But ADHD souls crave meaning, passion, and **connection beyond structure**.

They may struggle with repetitive prayers or rituals — but excel at **spontaneous gratitude, deep empathy, and awe**.

They may forget formal teachings — but never forget **how someone made them feel**.

In Jewish tradition, there's room for this too.
The Baal Shem Tov taught that a broken heart and simple yearning may reach further than polished words.
King David himself cried out from chaos — and his Psalms became eternal.

ADHD adults can develop **spiritual paths of honesty and raw connection**, even if it doesn't follow a traditional script.

Healing the Narrative

Many ADHD adults carry a **lifetime of criticism**.

From teachers:
"You're not living up to your potential."

From bosses:
"You're difficult to manage."

From partners:
"You don't pull your weight."

From themselves:
"I can't do anything right."

This narrative becomes a **wound**. A lens through which they see everything.

But here's the truth:

- ADHD is not a moral failing.
- You are not broken.
- You were not meant to be someone else.

The healing begins when we **rewrite the story**.

Not "I am a failure," but:

"I have a different operating system. I now choose to learn how to use it."

Reclaiming Strength

Adults with ADHD are:

- Innovators
- Entrepreneurs

- Artists
- Educators
- Problem-solvers
- Healers

They thrive in motion, under pressure, in creativity, in crisis, in curiosity.

They are not "too much" — they are often **exactly what the world needs**.

When we support them, understand them, and empower them they build, connect, lead, inspire.

The work isn't easy—but the reward? It's worth it: clarity, owning your story, and finally living a life that fits.
I know this from experience. As a kid I just didn't feel like I belonged. I was reading adult-books, not really into what everyone else my age was into, and neither they nor I understood why. I had only two or three friends (and hey — you know who you are — thanks for sticking with me).
I was pulled toward adult friendships (which, yeah, back-fired at times). Some adults thought I was really smart and "right on"—others? They thought I was weird. They'd ask, "Why can't we talk about sports or things people your age care about?"

(And just to be clear: this isn't about my childhood illnesses — meningitis and encephalitis — this is about the deeper feeling of not fitting in, because my (undiagnosed ADHD).

An other part is that this feeling might lead for people to want to escape realty Like drugs and alcohol also even though negative attention it gives ATTENTION ! or even stealing or other things just to belong and fit in with others thank God this was not my issue but I have seen it by others in my environment, just a reminder, ADHD'ers attracked each other since we are wired similar like the multi tasking and way of thinking. This could be good or bad.

Chapter 7: The Role of the Support System — No One Thrives Alone

"I always thought I had to do it all myself. It took me 40 years to realize: I wasn't broken — I was unsupported."

The journey with ADHD, perhaps more than any other neurodivergent condition, highlights one vital truth: **No one thrives alone.** Behind every thriving adult with ADHD is a support system — visible or hidden — that provides structure, belief, boundaries, compassion, and accountability.

In this chapter, we explore what a healthy support system looks like, how to build one, how to become part of someone else's, and what happens when the system fails — or is never there to begin with.

The Myth of the Lone Fighter

From a young age, many individuals with ADHD receive subtle or direct messages like:

- "Figure it out."

- "You're smart, you don't need help."
- "Why can't you be like your sister?"
- "Stop making excuses."

These messages embed shame. Over time, many with ADHD learn to **mask** their struggles. They compensate through overachievement, people-pleasing, or becoming clowns to cover pain.

But masking takes its toll. It drains energy and reinforces a destructive belief:

"If I just tried harder, I'd be fine."

This belief isolates. It keeps individuals from seeking support — even when they are drowning. The truth is the opposite: **ADHD is not a character flaw — it's a difference in brain wiring.** And no one with ADHD is meant to walk alone.

What is a Support System?

A support system is not just about having friends or family. It's a **deliberate circle of roles** — each one offering a different kind of help.

A strong ADHD support system includes:

1. **Emotional Anchors**
   People who love and accept you unconditionally. They listen without judgment and provide a safe place to land after setbacks.

2. **Structural Guides**
   Individuals who help create external order: setting reminders, organizing calendars, building routines, managing paperwork.

3. **Accountability Partners**
   Those who help track progress toward goals — not by shaming, but by gently checking in and reminding.

4. **Mentors and Coaches**
   People who see your potential, guide your growth, and offer tools you haven't yet mastered.

5. **Medical and Mental Health Professionals**
   Psychiatrists, therapists, neurologists, or general doctors who understand ADHD and can prescribe, educate, or guide treatment.

6. **Community Support**
   ADHD support groups (online or in person), neurodivergent communities, faith-based networks — places where you're not "the only one."

7. **Workplace Allies**
   Supervisors, co-workers, or HR partners who understand your challenges and help shape your work environment to fit your brain.

Each of these roles **adds one more layer of stability** to a life often marked by internal and external chaos.

Family: The First (and Often Most Fragile) Layer

Family can be a powerful asset — or a source of deep harm.

When a child with ADHD grows up in a supportive family, they learn:

- Mistakes are opportunities, not verdicts.
- Routines and structure are grounding, not punishment.
- Emotions can be intense but manageable.
- Help is a tool, not a weakness.

But in many homes, especially where ADHD is not understood, families respond with:

- Criticism ("Why can't you just do it?")
- Comparisons ("Your brother can manage fine.")

- Shame ("You're always the problem.")
- Control ("If I don't micromanage you, you'll fall apart.")

These patterns crush confidence and drive people into isolation. Adults who grew up in such environments often fear vulnerability, dismiss their needs, and suffer in silence.

Healing requires re-learning:

"My needs are real. I deserve support. And I'm allowed to ask for help."

Romantic Partners: Love, Frustration, and Shared Growth

A romantic partner can be the most important member of an ADHD support system — but also the most strained.

Living with someone with ADHD can feel, at times, like living with a whirlwind.
They may:

- Start projects and not finish them
- Leave things half-done
- Forget plans

- Interrupt often
- Shift moods quickly

Without understanding, a partner may interpret these actions as laziness, carelessness, or emotional volatility.

Over time, resentment builds. The non-ADHD partner may feel like they've become a parent, not a partner.

To avoid collapse, couples must **understand ADHD together.**

Successful ADHD couples build:

- Shared calendars
- Non-judgmental communication strategies
- Agreements around roles and tasks
- Recognition of effort, not just results

Importantly, the ADHD partner must **own their part** and work to grow — but not alone. The non-ADHD partner must avoid **becoming the entire system**. No one should carry that burden alone.

Friendships That Hold You Together

ADHD can make friendships harder to maintain:

- Forgetting to reply
- Showing up late
- Talking too much or zoning out
- Being "too much" or "too intense"
- Disappearing during burnout

As a result, many adults with ADHD carry deep friendship wounds. They fear they are a "bad friend," and may isolate out of shame.

But when real friends understand — and stay — they become **life-giving**.

A good friend doesn't need to be your therapist or coach. Their gift is **presence, belief, patience** — and reminding you who you are when you forget.

The Role of Faith and Spiritual Community

Faith communities — when healthy — can play a profound role in supporting people with ADHD.

They offer:

- **Rituals and structure** (Shabbat, prayers, holidays, etc.)

- **Purpose and grounding**
- **Belonging** without performance
- **Chesed and support networks**
- **Models of forgiveness and renewal**

In many traditions, spiritual figures were themselves intense, sensitive, or even impulsive — from King David to prophets and mystics. Their depth came not in spite of their emotional intensity, but through it.

In Judaism, the Baal Shem Tov taught:

"God desires the heart."

Not perfection. Not stillness. But honesty.

When a person with ADHD finds spiritual spaces where their **inner world is welcomed**, it becomes part of their support — even their healing.

Professional Help is Not a Sign of Weakness

Therapists. Coaches. Doctors. ADHD specialists.

These people can help with:

- **Medication** that actually fits your needs

- **Executive function strategies**

- **CBT** to deal with shame, anxiety, and rejection sensitivity

- **Parent training** if you're raising a child with ADHD

- **Diagnosis clarity** if you've never been officially evaluated

Unfortunately, many adults still feel embarrassed to reach out.
They say things like:

- "I should be able to handle this."

- "It's too late now."

- "What can a coach really do?"

But support professionals are trained to **cut through the fog** — not to do the work for you, but to walk with you while you learn to do it better.

Therapy and coaching don't fix ADHD. But they make **living with ADHD not just manageable — but meaningful.**

What Happens Without Support

Without a support system, the adult with ADHD often experiences:

- **Burnout** from trying to manage everything alone
- **Depression** from chronic failure and shame
- **Anxiety** from constantly missing deadlines or forgetting things
- **Relationship strain** from being misunderstood
- **Financial instability** from disorganization and impulsivity
- **Loss of self-trust** after years of internalized criticism

Many reach a breaking point.

And yet, most still don't ask for help — because they believe the lie:

"It's my fault. I should have tried harder."

This chapter is here to say clearly: **You were never meant to carry this alone.**

How to Build (or Rebuild) Your Support System

If your support system is broken, toxic, or nonexistent — you're not doomed. You can start rebuilding, one brick at a time.

1. **Start with One Safe Person**
   Someone you trust. Someone who doesn't shame you. Start talking.

2. **Educate Your Inner Circle**
   Share articles. Invite them to join sessions. Help them see ADHD clearly.

3. **Seek ADHD-Specific Support**
   Join a support group. Follow a podcast. Read stories of others like you.

4. **Invest in One Professional Ally**
   A therapist, coach, or ADHD-informed doctor.

5. **Simplify Your Circle**
   Some people won't get it — and that's okay. You don't need to justify your brain to everyone.

6. **Say the Hard Thing**
   "I need help."
   "I don't know how to do this alone."
   "Can we work together on a system?"

Every step forward strengthens your structure.

Becoming a Support to Others

If you love someone with ADHD, you might wonder:

"How can I help without enabling?"
"How do I support without becoming exhausted?"

Here are guidelines:

- **Ask, don't assume** – "What would support look like for you?"

- **Praise effort** – not just outcomes.

- **Set boundaries** – your needs matter too.

- **Avoid moralizing** – they're not lazy or bad. Their brain works differently.

- **Stay consistent** – even when they're not.

- **Celebrate small wins** – sometimes, getting out of bed is heroic.

Your belief in them **may be the bridge** they walk over to believe in themselves.

In Jewish Thought: The Chavrusa Model

In traditional Torah learning, no one learns alone. Every student has a **chavrusa** — a study partner.

The chavrusa challenges, listens, encourages, and holds them accountable.
The goal isn't perfection — but **sharpening through relationship**.

So too with ADHD. The brain may wander. But when tethered to another human who walks with compassion and clarity — that brain can fly.

Closing Thought: From Isolation to Integration

Support isn't weakness.
Support isn't pity.
Support is **human design**.

Everyone — neurotypical or not — is shaped by the quality of their relationships.

For those with ADHD, the need is simply more visible.
More urgent.
More sacred.

If you're walking alone — stop.
Look around. Reach out. Build. Rebuild.

And if you're part of someone's journey — stay. Listen. Learn. Offer kindness that **frees** rather than controls.

A village doesn't just raise a child.
Sometimes, it **rescues the adult they became**.

Chapter 8: What the World Gets Wrong About ADHD

Myths Debunked — From Stigma and Shame to Empowerment and Advocacy

"But you're so smart. You can't have ADHD."
"Everyone's a little ADHD sometimes."
"You just need to try harder."
"That diagnosis is just an excuse for bad parenting."

We've all heard them — the throwaway comments, the judgmental tones, the well-meaning but harmful advice. The experience of living with ADHD is not just defined by what happens inside the brain — it's also shaped, and often warped, by how the world responds to it.

This chapter is about clearing the fog. Tearing down myths. Replacing blame with understanding. And most of all — moving from shame to self-worth, from hiding to advocacy.

Because what the world gets wrong about ADHD has cost too many people too much for far too long.

Part I: The Dangerous Myths About ADHD

Myth #1: ADHD Is Just an Excuse for Laziness

This is one of the most harmful and widespread misunderstandings. It assumes that the person with ADHD could succeed — if only they'd try harder. But research has shown time and again that ADHD is not a *motivation* disorder — it's a *regulation* disorder. Most people with ADHD *want* to succeed. They're often painfully aware of their missed opportunities.

The truth: ADHD impairs executive functions — the brain's ability to prioritize, plan, begin tasks, persist through boredom, and switch between ideas. It's not about *not caring*. It's about *not being able to activate consistently*.

The internal experience is often:

"I know what I need to do. I want to do it. But I can't start."

That's not laziness. That's neurology.

Myth #2: ADHD Is a Childhood Problem

Too many people assume that ADHD is something kids "grow out of." This results in underdiagnosis of adults — especially those who managed to mask their symptoms in school.

The truth: ADHD is a lifelong neurological difference. While hyperactivity may lessen with age, issues like disorganization, time blindness, impulsivity, and mental restlessness often persist — and even worsen under adult pressures (career, relationships, parenting).

Many adults are only diagnosed in their 30s, 40s, or even 60s — after years of unexplained struggle, self-doubt, and misdiagnoses (like depression or anxiety).

Myth #3: ADHD Is Overdiagnosed

This myth is based more on media headlines than reality. Critics often cite rising diagnosis rates as proof that ADHD is a "fad." But what we're actually seeing is a *correction* of years of underdiagnosis — especially among girls, minorities, and adults.

The truth: ADHD is still **underdiagnosed** in many populations — particularly in women, people of color, and older adults.

Additionally, many who *are* diagnosed never receive adequate treatment or accommodations.

Overdiagnosis is far less common than misdiagnosis (e.g., anxiety or bipolar disorder being mistaken for ADHD — and vice versa).

Myth #4: ADHD Equals Hyperactivity

The stereotypical image of ADHD is a young boy bouncing off walls. This narrow view ignores the full spectrum of ADHD presentations.

The truth:
ADHD comes in three types:
- Predominantly inattentive
- Predominantly hyperactive-impulsive
- Combined type

Many with ADHD — especially girls — are daydreamers, not disruptors. They appear quiet, polite, even "gifted," while inwardly battling mental chaos. These individuals often go undetected and unsupported.

Myth #5: Medication Is a Quick Fix

Some assume that stimulant medication is a magic cure, or conversely, that it's a dangerous crutch. Both views are oversimplifications.

The truth:
Medication is a tool — not a cure. For many, it provides a foundation: increased focus, reduced impulsivity, and better emotional regulation. But it often works best *with* therapy, coaching, lifestyle changes, and structure.

When prescribed responsibly, ADHD medication is one of the most studied and effective psychiatric treatments in modern medicine.

Myth #6: People With ADHD Can't Be Successful

This myth is shattered daily by the lives of countless high-achieving individuals with ADHD. Yet the narrative persists — especially in schools and workplaces — leading to underestimation, mistreatment, and burnout.

The truth:
ADHD doesn't prevent success. But it can make the *path* to success longer, messier, and more emotionally exhausting — especially without support.

Famous people with ADHD include:

- Simone Biles (Olympic gymnast)
- Michael Phelps (Olympic swimmer)

- Richard Branson (business magnate)
- Will Smith (actor)
- Albert Einstein (speculatively posthumously described with ADHD traits)

Their success is not *despite* ADHD — but often because of traits *linked* to ADHD: risk-taking, creativity, persistence, and visionary thinking.

Part II: The Cost of Misunderstanding

Stigma: The Silent Saboteur

ADHD carries a unique stigma: "not sick enough to need help, but too scattered to function normally." This in-between place creates shame.

People internalize failure, seeing it as moral weakness. They hide their diagnosis. They fake normalcy. They burn out — alone.

Workplaces may label them as unreliable. Teachers may label them as lazy. Families may label them as selfish. None of these labels are true — but all of them are heavy.

Stigma delays diagnosis. It discourages treatment. It pushes people into isolation.

Shame: The Invisible Wound

Shame is a shadow that follows many ADHD lives. It starts young:

- "Why can't you just sit still?"
- "Why did you forget again?"
- "Why are you always so emotional?"

And it continues:

- "Why did I miss another deadline?"
- "Why can't I keep a relationship?"
- "Why can't I finish anything?"

Shame doesn't motivate. It paralyzes.

For many, the hardest part of ADHD isn't the disorganization — it's the constant fear of disappointing everyone, including themselves.

Misdiagnosis and Misunderstanding

Without proper understanding, ADHD is often mistaken for:

- Depression
- Anxiety
- Bipolar disorder
- Personality disorders
- Oppositional defiant disorder (in children)

This leads to inappropriate treatments — or worse, a sense of "nothing works," when in reality, the right treatment hasn't been tried.

Part III: From Shame to Strength — Rewriting the Narrative

Empowerment Begins with Education

Understanding ADHD is the first step toward reclaiming one's story. When individuals learn:

- *"I'm not lazy, I have a wiring difference,"*

- *"I'm not broken, I'm creative and divergent,"*
- *"There are tools that can help,"*

...their entire self-perception changes.

Families, too, begin to shift. Teachers become allies. Workplaces become more inclusive.

Advocacy as a Healing Act

Speaking openly about ADHD — whether on social media, in the workplace, or within families — helps deconstruct stigma. It also gives others the courage to seek help.

Advocacy isn't just political. It's personal. It's saying:

- "I have ADHD, and I'm proud of how far I've come."
- "We all learn and live differently — and that's okay."

Even just *telling your story* can be a revolution.

Building ADHD-Friendly Environments

Schools and employers can do better. Here's how:

In Education:

- Flexible deadlines
- Movement breaks
- Executive function coaching
- Access to fidget tools and alternate seating
- Training for teachers in neurodiversity

In Workplaces:

- Clear expectations
- Written and verbal instructions
- Regular feedback
- Quiet zones
- Flexible scheduling

These changes don't just benefit people with ADHD — they create a more humane environment for everyone.

Reclaiming Self-Worth

To thrive with ADHD is to *dismantle the lies*:

- That you're not trying hard enough
- That you don't care
- That you're too much
- That you'll never get it together

And to replace them with truths:

- That your brain is wired for bursts, not steadiness
- That your emotions run deep — and that's beautiful
- That your passion is power
- That support isn't weakness, it's wisdom

Final Thoughts: The World Needs What ADHD Offers

In a world addicted to order, people with ADHD bring spark.
In a world afraid of change, they bring innovation.
In a world that moves slowly, they bring urgency.

Yes, ADHD can hurt. It can exhaust. But it also creates artists, entrepreneurs, healers, inventors, and revolutionaries.

What the world gets wrong about ADHD isn't just a misunderstanding — it's a missed opportunity.

Let us be the generation that gets it right.

Sub chapter 8b Faith, Focus, and Function — Reconnecting the Inner Compass

ADHD is not just a neurological condition; it is a journey that can feel like wandering through a fog with a hyperactive compass. Thoughts leap, emotions crash like waves, and even with the best of intentions, the person finds themselves derailed, again and again. In this chapter, we explore how **faith** — in G-d, in self, or in something higher — can restore **focus**, and how true focus can enable **function**, transforming chaos into creation.

1. The Fractured Lens

A person with ADHD often perceives the world through a shattered lens. Focus comes in bursts, and direction feels elusive. The traditional model of cause and effect, effort and reward, seems skewed. Tasks that seem simple to others — getting up, answering emails, cleaning a room — feel overwhelming. And in the mind of someone with ADHD, this disconnect quickly translates into shame: *"Why can't I just do what everyone else seems to manage so easily?"

Shame clouds clarity. A person struggling internally begins to lose trust not only in others, but in themselves. Without trust, focus collapses. And without focus, function breaks.

This is where faith becomes more than theology. It becomes a **lifeline**.

2. Faith: The Anchor in the Storm

Faith does not mean ignoring reality. On the contrary, it means trusting that reality has layers deeper than what the eye can see. For many, this begins with belief in G-d, or in a divine plan. For others, it's the faith that there is purpose in their wiring, that their mind is not broken, just differently designed.

Faith creates **internal permission** to try again. To forgive oneself. To believe that there is a path, even if it twists and turns. It says:

*"I may not function like others, but I am not lesser. I am designed for something unique."

Faith is also about letting go. Many with ADHD are perfectionists at heart. They want so badly to succeed that failure becomes unbearable. Faith allows one to release that control and to say, *"Hashem, I will do my part; the rest is Yours."*

This is not passivity. It is partnership. Emunah doesn't replace effort — it enhances it by grounding it.

3. Focus: From Scattered to Sacred

Focus is often misunderstood in the ADHD world. It's not that the person cannot focus; it's that they focus on everything or the wrong thing at the wrong time. Or they hyperfocus on one thing and lose the rest.

When faith is present, focus becomes **directed**. The heart stops racing. The mind stops resisting. Why? Because there is clarity. When the soul feels safe, the mind feels safe to choose one thing.

Tools that help sharpen this include:

- **Prayer or Meditation** — quieting the noise
- **Mindful scheduling** — allowing space between tasks

- **Accountability partners** — someone to reflect back what's real

- **Purpose-oriented planning** — not just "what do I need to do?" but "why?"

Once we align our attention with our intention, focus blossoms. And focus, when tied to meaning, becomes sacred.

4. Function: When the Soul and the Brain Shake Hands

Function is not the ability to perform like others. It is the ability to perform **as oneself**. When someone with ADHD tries to conform to neurotypical standards, they often collapse. But when they are empowered to function *in line with their nature*, incredible things happen.

Faith creates stability. Focus brings clarity. Function arises when those two combine.

For example, a person who cannot sit still may thrive in a job that requires movement. One who forgets appointments may become a master of spontaneous creativity. The key is not to force the square peg into the round hole, but to build a square socket.

In halacha (Jewish law), function is also measured by intention. A mitzvah done without kavana (intention) may not fulfill its purpose. This mirrors the ADHD journey: performance is not enough — there must be presence.

5. Spiritual Tools for Functional Living

Here are a few tools rooted in both Torah and universal wisdom:

- **Modeh Ani with Presence**: Start the day by saying the morning prayer *Modeh Ani* with full awareness. This centers the soul before the mind races.

- **Kavanah Checkpoints**: Pause before major tasks and ask, *"What is my deeper why here?"

- **Daily Teshuvah (Return)**: Every evening, reflect without judgment. What went well? What can I adjust tomorrow? Teshuvah is not guilt — it's guidance.

- **Tefillah as Focus Training**: Davening with sincerity — even for 3 minutes — is a gym for attention.

- **Chavrusa or Coaching**: Torah is learned in partnership for a reason. The same applies to life.

6. Stories of Reconnection

- **Miriam**, a young woman with ADHD, failed out of three colleges. Only when she reframed her struggle as part of a bigger mission — to help others like her — did she find focus. She now runs a mentoring program for girls with executive dysfunction.

- **Ezra**, a father of five, constantly forgot errands and mismanaged his time. But after embracing a simple 3-minute morning prayer routine and setting one goal per day, he found calm. His children say he became more present. "You hear us now, Abba," they told him.

- **Yaakov**, a yeshiva student, was mocked for his restlessness. His rosh yeshiva told him to take walk-breaks while reviewing Gemara. Yaakov ended up writing a commentary on masechet Brachot while hiking. His "disorder" became his gateway.

7. From Surviving to Serving

Ultimately, ADHD is not an excuse nor a curse. It is a different **starting point** on the journey of becoming. Faith anchors that journey. Focus channels it. Function fulfills it.

Let no one say to an Addie, "You are not capable." Rather let the world say:

"You were given a different soul-compass. May your steps be guided by faith, your eyes fixed in focus, and your hands engaged in function. "Because in the hands of someone aligned, ADHD becomes not a dysfunction — but a sacred force.

Chapter 9: Building a Personalized ADHD Strategy

Daily Planner Methods, Time-Blocking for Impulsive Minds, and the Power of Self-Talk Introduction: Why Strategy Matters More for the Neurodivergent Mind

Living with ADHD is like driving a racecar with bicycle brakes. Speed is never the issue. Direction, timing, and focus are. For those with ADHD, traditional productivity methods often fall short because they weren't designed for minds that sprint, leap, and detour by design. In this chapter, we will explore a new approach to planning and self-regulation — one tailored to the impulsive, imaginative, often nonlinear brilliance of the ADHD brain.

Section 1: The ADHD Brain Needs Structure — But Flexible Structure

Many with ADHD recoil from the idea of strict routines and rigid systems. And rightly so. These often feel like chains instead of supports. Yet, paradoxically, the ADHD brain craves a **framework** — a skeleton to hold the day together, as long as it allows some freedom to breathe.

The solution lies in **personalized structure**: daily systems that are fluid but not chaotic, firm but not suffocating. This balance begins with tools like:

- Visual cues

- Short-term rewards

- Color-coded systems

- Digital or paper planners that align with the user's instincts

Rather than asking the ADHD brain to "act neurotypical," these strategies work *with* the natural rhythm and energy spikes of the person.

Section 2: Daily Planner Methods for the ADHD Brain

A. Bullet Journals with Structure

The ADHD version of bullet journaling is more than a trend; it's a lifeline. Instead of lengthy descriptions, use:

- Symbols (✓ for done, → for moved, for in progress)
- Daily "focus of the day" — one central task to anchor you
- Weekly brain-dump pages: no order, just get it out
- Mood and habit trackers for emotional awareness

B. Time-Themed Planners

- **AM/PM Priority Blocks** — List your top 3 tasks per half-day. That's it.

- **Energy-Based Planning** — Match tasks to your natural rhythm (e.g., creative writing in the morning, calls in the afternoon).

- **Theme Days** — Monday = errands, Tuesday = deep work, etc.

C. Visual Wall Calendars and Kanban Boards

Externalizing your tasks and days onto walls or boards works wonders. It eliminates the "where was I supposed to be?" syndrome and gives dopamine hits as you move tasks from "To Do" → "Doing" → "Done."

Section 3: Time-Blocking for Impulsive Minds

Time-blocking often fails for ADHD users — but not because the idea is bad. It's the rigidity that kills it.

ADHD-Friendly Time-Blocking Tips:

- **Micro-blocks:** Instead of 2-hour chunks, use 20–30 minute "focus pods."

- **Floating Flex Blocks:** Leave 1–2 blocks daily for unexpected needs or ADHD tangents.

- **Visual Timers:** Use sand timers, phone alarms, or Pomodoro apps that show time passing.

- **Bookend Your Day:** Always block the **start** (wake-up, plan, move body) and **end** (wind down, journal, prep for next day). That's your anchor.

Example:

Time	Task	Notes
8:00–8:30	Morning movement + coffee	No phone until after
9:00–9:30	Priority Task: Email replies	Use a timer
9:30–10:00	Free time/flex	Impulse block
10:00–10:30	Deep work block	Phone in drawer
11:00–12:00	Meetings or errands	Pre-set routes

Section 4: Self-Talk, Journaling, and ADHD-Friendly Apps

The inner dialogue of someone with ADHD can be brutal: "Why can't I just do this?" "I'm lazy." "What's wrong with me?" These narratives create more harm than the ADHD itself.

A. Power of Self-Talk

We must **reframe** the internal voice. Try these ADHD-aligned affirmations:

- "I'm doing my best with the brain Hashem gave me."

- "A late start is still a start."
- "Progress over perfection."
- "Today I win by showing up."

Use **name-based talk** for grounding: "David, right now your job is just to begin."

B. Journaling for the ADHD Soul

Journaling builds **external memory** — critical for ADHD. Formats that help:

- **Daily brain-dumps**: No order. Just write.
- **Top 3 wins of the day**: Reframe with positivity.
- **Next steps**: Not full to-dos. Just the *next* micro-action.
- **Emotion + Trigger Tracker**: Helps notice patterns.

C. Apps That Actually Work for ADHD Users

1. **Todoist** – Clean, priority-based list with due dates.
2. **Trello** – Visual kanban boards for projects.
3. **Time Timer** – Visual clock for time awareness.

4. **Notion** – Fully customizable planner and database for advanced users.

5. **Daylio** – Track mood + activities without typing.

Each app should be **set up by someone else or during high-focus time** — setup fatigue often kills ADHD app use.

Section 5: Building Your Custom Routine — a Living Document

The ADHD strategy is never "set and forget." It is a living, evolving plan. Check in weekly:

- What worked?
- What felt like a grind?
- What small win can I repeat next week?

Create a *"Success Formula Template"*:

1. I start my day best when I...
2. My triggers for distraction are...
3. My best productivity tool is...
4. My support team includes...

5. My brain feels best when I...

6. I need to remember that...

Print it. Fill it out monthly. Watch yourself evolve.

Conclusion: ADHD Strategy Is Self-Compassion in Action

This chapter is not about discipline. It's about dignity. It's about creating a world where your ADHD can function not *despite* itself, but *through* its own unique brilliance.

By using personalized planners, embracing flexible time-blocking, and building a loving internal dialogue, you craft not just a strategy, but a **daily act of self-respect**.

The ADHD brain isn't broken. It's just untrained for the wrong system.

Let's give it the system it deserves.

If you've made it this far, you already know ADHD is not a one-size-fits-all condition. It's a spectrum. A dance of electricity across the brain. A storm in some, a whirlwind in others, and in a few — a quietly flickering light trying to be seen. So how do you build a plan that works? Not a generic "Top 10 Tips" list, but a strategy tailored to *you*?

This chapter helps you lay the foundation. Not by prescribing another system for you to fail at, but by giving you the tools to build your own — one that grows with you, not against you.

Chapter 10: relationships, ADHD, and the Challenge of Connection:

1. Know Your Type

Start by identifying how ADHD shows up in your life. Are you:

- The daydreamer who gets lost in your own thoughts?
- The bouncer who can't sit still or stop interrupting?
- The hyper-focused night owl who forgets to eat but remembers obscure details from 10 years ago?

Understanding *your* ADHD flavor helps determine the tools you need. There's no shame in the label — the shame is in not using it to your advantage.

2. The Three Pillars: Focus, Function, Flexibility

Most successful ADHD strategies rest on three legs:

Focus

This is your ability to engage with a task, block distractions, and complete something — even something you hate. It's where timers, playlists, and intentional workspace design come in.

Try:

- Pomodoro method (25-min work / 5-min break)
- Lo-fi music or binaural beats
- Noise-canceling headphones
- Visual task boards like Kanban or Trello

Function

How do you organize your daily life? Keys, bills, appointments — the stuff that melts when we're overwhelmed. Functional strategies are the glue that keep ADHDers from unraveling.

Try:

- Color-coded calendars
- Weekly meal prep or clothing rotation
- A designated place for everything (yes, *everything*)
- Automate where possible: bill pay, reminders, medication refills

Flexibility

ADHD'ers crash when their system is too rigid. Life changes. Mood shifts. Energy fluctuates. Your plan must breathe with you.

Try:

- A "Catch-Up Day" every week
- A backup "Plan B" when you feel off
- Building buffer time into your schedule
- Keeping your to-do list limited to 3 must-do items per day

3. Time-Blocking for the ADHD Brain

Time doesn't feel the same when you have ADHD. Ten minutes can vanish. Three hours can feel like two. So time-blocking is not just useful — it's lifesaving.

Traditional vs. ADHD Time-Blocking

- **Traditional:** 8 AM – 9 AM = Emails. 9–10 = Project A.

- **ADHD Style:**
  - Block by **mode**, not by task.
  - "Brainstorming time," "Admin time," "Creative focus," "Errands + movement."
  - Align blocks to your energy. If your brain is slow in the morning, don't plan your most focused work then.

Create a daily flow that mirrors your energy waves, not a military schedule. Use colors, stickers, visuals — anything that makes the abstract visible.

4. Morning & Evening Anchors

ADHD lives in chaos when there's no structure. You don't need 14 rigid habits. You need two anchors: **morning** and **evening**.

Morning Ritual:

- Wake up at a consistent time
- Water + light
- One non-negotiable task (make bed, weigh in, stretch)
- Review your top 3 priorities for the day

Evening Wind-Down:

- Brain dump — write tomorrow's thoughts tonight
- Prepare clothing, bag, food for tomorrow
- Set a bedtime alarm *before* you're overtired
- No screens 30–60 minutes before sleep

These routines are not just productivity hacks — they protect your brain from overwhelm and shutdown.

5. Self-Talk, Journaling, and Cognitive Rewiring

ADHD comes with a harsh inner critic. Years of being told "you're lazy," "you're not trying," or "you always mess up" creates a script in the mind. Break that script.

Try:

- Daily journaling: Just one paragraph
- Reframing: "I'm not lazy — my executive function is overloaded"
- Post-it notes with positive scripts:
    - "Progress, not perfection"
    - "Done is better than perfect"
    - "I am not my productivity"

The goal is not just better performance — it's better *peace*.

6. Medication and Nutrition

For many ADHD'ers, medication can be part of the strategy — but it's not the whole strategy.

- If you're on medication, treat it like glasses: it helps you *see*, but you still need to know how to read.

- If you're not on meds, lifestyle changes — like high-protein breakfasts, avoiding sugar crashes, and good sleep hygiene — become even more crucial.

Supplements, Omega-3s, and blood sugar management may all be supportive, but always consult a doctor or specialist.

7. Your Personal "ADHD Dashboard"

Create a visual dashboard of your brain.

You can include:

- Weekly planner

- Mood tracker

- Goal chart

- Reward system

- "Oops List" — patterns of what tends to go wrong (forgetting appointments, overbooking, underestimating time)

Make it **visual**. ADHD doesn't like hidden data. Your mind responds to what it can *see*.

8. Accountability: The Secret Weapon

The ADHD brain craves **urgency** and **connection**. Without accountability, tasks drift endlessly.

Options:

- Body double (someone working near you)

- Check-in texts with a friend or coach

- Visual progress charts

- Group support — in person or online

You're more likely to follow through when someone is waiting on you. Even if it's your cat.

9. Celebrate Small Wins

ADHD makes people forget how far they've come. Start tracking wins — daily, weekly, monthly.

- Did you do your morning routine three days this week? ✓
- Did you sit through a meeting without biting your tongue off? ✓
- Did you send that email you avoided for 5 days? ✓

Each one matters. You don't build a mountain with one boulder. You do it with **gravel** — one small, gritty, faithful win at a time.

10. Your Strategy Will Change — and That's Okay

Don't fall in love with your first system. Or your tenth. The key is to **adapt**, not to rigidly cling to what no longer works.

Just like your brain, your strategy is meant to evolve. Expect setbacks. Expect bad weeks. But build systems that help you **bounce back**, not just succeed.

Final Words

Building a personalized ADHD strategy isn't about fixing yourself. It's about understanding how your brain works and creating a life that works with it — not against it. You're not broken. You're differently wired. And with the right tools, support, and self-kindness, you can build a system that honors both your struggle and your brilliance.

Let your strategy be an act of *chesed* — kindness — to your future self.

Chapter 11 : Relationships, ADHD, and the Challenge of Connection

Love, Friendship, and Family Through the ADHD Lens

Introduction: Loving With an ADHD Brain

ADHD doesn't just affect deadlines and desks — it affects hearts. Whether it's friendship, family, marriage, or dating, the ADHD brain brings a unique mix of intensity, spontaneity, distraction, forgetfulness, deep loyalty, and misunderstood behavior.

Relationships are where the blessings and curses of ADHD collide. But with understanding, tools, and love, ADHD can enrich connections rather than unravel them.

Section 1: How ADHD Affects Emotional Bonds

A. Rejection Sensitivity Dysphoria (RSD)

Many people with ADHD experience extreme emotional pain at perceived rejection or criticism — even if none was intended. This RSD leads to:

- Emotional outbursts
- Withdrawal and shutdowns
- Over-apologizing or over-pleasing
- Relationship sabotage out of fear

Understanding RSD is key to building compassion for oneself and for loved ones.

B. Memory Gaps in Relationships

It's not personal. It's neurological.

ADHD makes it hard to hold onto dates, promises, or even things someone just said. This can lead to the accusation: "You don't care."

In truth, it's not a lack of care — it's a lack of **working memory**. People with ADHD may love intensely but forget to call.

C. Hyperfocus: The Double-Edged Sword

In the early stages of love, someone with ADHD may enter hyperfocus — becoming completely absorbed in the other person.

It feels magical — but when the brain shifts out of hyperfocus, the partner might feel abandoned.

This isn't deception. It's neurological ebb and flow. The key is to **balance emotion with structure**.

Section 2: ADHD in Marriage and Long-Term Partnerships

A. Common ADHD Relationship Cycles

- One partner feels like the "parent"; the other like the "child"
- Resentment builds: "Why can't you just…?"
- Chores and responsibilities are unevenly split
- ADHD partner feels misunderstood; non-ADHD partner feels alone

B. Strategies for Harmony

1. **Clarity over assumptions** – ADHD minds often misread tone. Speak clearly and kindly.
2. **Use reminders lovingly** – A sticky note isn't nagging. It's helping.
3. **Appreciate strengths** – Creativity, spontaneity, humor, deep passion.

4. **Couples therapy with ADHD education** – A therapist who understands ADHD makes all the difference.

5. **Assign roles by strengths** – Let the ADHD spouse handle the creative, spontaneous, or fast-paced tasks.

C. Emotional Intimacy and Vulnerability

ADHD partners can be deeply loving but afraid of being "too much" or "not enough." Emotional safety means:

- Letting them stim, move, or fidget during hard conversations
- Giving space without punishment
- Reassurance that forgetfulness ≠ indifference

Section 3: Parenting With (or a Child With) ADHD

A. ADHD Parent: The Rollercoaster Mom or Dad

ADHD parents may:

- Forget permission slips, but create magical birthdays

- Miss deadlines, but invent bedtime songs

- Be inconsistent, yet deeply loving

Tip: Use systems to create consistency and get outside help for structure.

B. Raising an ADHD Child

The most powerful thing you can give your ADHD child is **understanding**.

- Don't punish impulsivity — teach emotional regulation

- Create structure, not shame

- Use rewards, not fear

- Build their identity around *strengths*, not just diagnosis

Section 4: Friendship and Social Life With ADHD

Friendship is often hard for those with ADHD due to:

- Interrupting

- Talking too much or zoning out

- Forgetting to respond or follow through
- Struggling to read social cues

But ADHD'ers are also:

- Loyal
- Passionate
- Fun
- Quick to forgive
- Deeply intuitive

Ways to Maintain Friendships:

- **Send short voice notes** instead of long texts
- **Set calendar pings** for birthdays and check-ins
- **Apologize with humility** when things slip
- **Explain your wiring** — "Sometimes I go quiet, but I care"
- **Choose friends who get it** — not everyone will

Section 5: Dating With ADHD

Dating while having ADHD is often described as:

"Feeling everything too much and too fast and then worrying if I said the wrong thing five hours later."

Tips for Successful ADHD Dating:

- **Be honest** about your ADHD, but don't lead with it
- **Choose quiet dates** where stimulation isn't overwhelming
- **Prepare scripts** for awkward or blank-mind moments
- **Avoid people who gaslight or shame your traits**
- **Use calendars to follow up** after good dates — even if you're not sure what to say

Section 6: Faith, Love, and the Spiritual Side of ADHD Connection

In many religious traditions, love is seen as a reflection of Divine unity — a place where opposites meet and become whole.

ADHD, with its contradiction and contrast, mirrors this. It brings:

- Depth in emotion
- Speed in devotion
- Frustration and forgiveness
- A heart that beats differently — but beats so loud, For Jewish readers: just as Hashem "remembers" His people despite their forgetfulness, so too must we learn to **hold love with grace**.

Conclusion: The Heart of ADHD Is Full of Love

ADHD doesn't prevent love — it intensifies it. It complicates connection but never kills it. With tools, honesty, and compassion, ADHD relationships can be **fierce, funny, deep, and loyal**.

The key isn't to "fix" the ADHD partner — it's to build bridges between brains. Because love isn't about being alike. It's about being *understood*.

Chapter 12: Workplace Realities

ADHD on the Job and in Career Choices

Introduction: When the Cubicle Doesn't Fit the Mind

Many people with ADHD have spent years being told they're " Too Much," "too distracted," or "not professional enough" for the workplace. But those same people often turn out to be the best innovators, problem-solvers, emergency responders, creative thinkers, and entrepreneurs — when placed in the right environment.

This chapter is not just about surviving at work with ADHD. It's about **choosing and shaping** careers that *fit the ADHD mind* — careers that ignite it rather than suppress it.

Section 1: The Myth of the Lazy Employee

ADHD does not mean lazy.

In fact, most adults with ADHD are constantly thinking, solving, fidgeting, worrying, planning, or running late because they *tried* to do too much.

But in a traditional office model — where punctuality, paper-trails, and passive compliance matter more than creative solutions — the ADHD employee may feel doomed.

Common ADHD Challenges at Work:

- Poor time estimation ("I thought I had more time...")
- Difficulty prioritizing
- Hyperfocus on the wrong task
- Paperwork overload
- Distractibility in open-plan offices
- Executive dysfunction: knowing what to do, but being unable to start

But here's the truth:

People with ADHD are often the **best people** to have in a crisis, under pressure, or when a system needs shaking up. The world needs that energy — it just has to be **channeled correctly**.

Section 2: Best Work Environments for ADHD Brains

ADHD-Friendly Workplaces Share These Traits:

- **Autonomy:** Room to make decisions or control one's schedule
- **Creativity:** Flexibility to think outside the box
- **Urgency:** Tight deadlines with fast-moving goals
- **Movement:** Physical jobs, or ones that include variety
- **Purpose:** Meaningful work that connects to identity

Examples of Good ADHD Career Fits:

- Emergency services (paramedic, firefighter)
- Teaching (especially creative, hands-on learning)
- Sales (especially commission-based or relationship-driven)
- Entrepreneurial ventures
- Counseling or coaching

- Performance arts or content creation
- Trades (electrician, builder, chef)
- Research and development roles
- IT troubleshooting or cybersecurity

Section 3: How to Navigate the Workplace with ADHD

A. Time Management Tools

- Use **visual calendars** and **color coding**
- Build in **double time estimates** to beat the "I'll be done in 10 minutes" fallacy
- Use **alarms for transitions**, not just tasks
- Create **buffer time** between meetings or deep work sessions

B. Emails and Communication

- Check emails 2–3 times per day — not continuously
- Use templates for frequent replies

- Record quick voice memos to yourself right after meetings

- Turn off notifications when focus is required

C. Physical Workspace Setup

- Face your desk away from traffic

- Use noise-canceling headphones or low music

- Keep only what you need for the task on your desk

- Use visual whiteboards or sticky notes over digital to-do apps if more effective

Section 4: Dealing with Criticism, Deadlines, and Authority

Many ADHD professionals struggle with feedback because of Rejection Sensitivity Dysphoria. Even light correction can feel like personal failure.

Tips to Handle Workplace Feedback:

- Request **written feedback** instead of face-to-face if you're sensitive

- Ask for **actionable items**, not vague criticisms

- Remind yourself: Feedback is a tool, not a sentence

- Use feedback to **refine systems**, not to judge yourself

Deadline Strategy:

- Break projects into *micro-steps* with *micro-deadlines*

- Share your deadlines publicly if external pressure helps

- Use accountability partners (coworker, app, mentor)

- Don't wait to feel "ready" — start the *first 3 minutes* of a task immediately

Section 5: Entrepreneurship and ADHD

ADHD individuals often shine as entrepreneurs, because:

- They think fast and take risks

- They pivot easily when something fails

- They see solutions where others see chaos

- They're passionate, driven, and hyper focused — when it's their dream

Keys to Success:

- **Delegate**: Get someone else to handle the paperwork, invoicing, and scheduling

- **Structure the freedom**: Use routines to anchor your creative chaos

- **Automate**: Email replies, financial reports, social media — automate what drains you

- **Partner up**: Many great ADHD entrepreneurs thrive with a grounded, neurotypical partner who handles the backend

Section 6: Legal Protections and Disclosure (US Focus)

In the United States, ADHD is recognized under the ADA (Americans with Disabilities Act), which means:

- You have a right to reasonable accommodations

- You do **not** have to disclose unless you want accommodations

- Accommodations may include extra time, flexible deadlines, noise-reduced spaces, written instructions

When to Disclose:

- If you're struggling and need support
- If your symptoms are misunderstood as performance issues
- If you're applying for accommodations in exams or licensing processes

Always **frame your ADHD as a strength with support needs**, not as a flaw.

Section 7: Spiritual View — A Mission in the Workplace

For those who draw inspiration from faith:

Every person is placed in a job for a reason. Even if it seems like you're not cut out for the job, perhaps the job is there to bring out your hidden strengths.

In Judaism, *parnassah* (livelihood) is a holy mission. Your job is not just a paycheck. It's a **tool for growth**. With

ADHD, your work may not look conventional — and that may be the whole point.

You were made to create paths where others follow maps.

Conclusion: The ADHD Mind Wasn't Made for the Assembly Line

The workplace of yesterday was designed for stillness, conformity, and silence. But the world is changing. Creativity, speed, adaptability, emotional intelligence, and intuition are **finally** being valued.

These are your strengths.

Whether you are an employee, manager, founder, artist, or helper — your job is to **work like yourself**.

Don't fake normal.
 Forge brilliance.

Chapter 13 : ADHD in the Classroom

Surviving and Thriving in School — For Students, Teachers, and Parents

Introduction: The Classroom — A Blessing or a Battlefield?

For many with ADHD, school is where the first wounds form. It's where they're labeled as "lazy," "disruptive," "too talkative," "not living up to potential." But it's also where the first sparks of brilliance often emerge — in a single creative project, a bold idea, or a surprising question no one else thought to ask.

This chapter explores how the classroom can either **crush** or **cultivate** the ADHD mind — and what students, parents, and educators can do to make it a place of thriving instead of just surviving.

Section 1: What School Feels Like for a Child With ADHD

Imagine sitting still for 7 hours a day while your brain screams for movement. Imagine being told "just focus" when your mind runs 1,000 tabs at once. That is the reality for many students with ADHD.

Common School Struggles:

- Difficulty focusing during long lectures
- Impulsively calling out answers or interrupting
- Trouble organizing materials or turning in homework
- Forgetting assignments, dates, and even what class they're in
- Social challenges — blurting, misreading cues, being seen as immature

And worst of all: being punished for a brain they cannot control.

Section 2: Reframing the Student's Identity

Before a student can succeed, they need to believe: **"I am not broken. I just learn differently."**

Too often, students internalize failure:

- "I'm dumb."
- "I'm lazy."
- "I'll never be good enough."

This leads to academic apathy, acting out, depression, or school refusal.

What Helps?

- Teachers who **focus on effort**, not just output
- Parents who **advocate fiercely** but never shame
- Systems that **reward creativity**, not only compliance
- Schools that **train staff** on executive function challenges and ADHD behavior

Section 3: School Strategies That Work

A. In the Classroom: For Teachers

1. **Movement Breaks** every 20–30 minutes (stretch, water, walk)

2. **Clear and visual instructions** — written + verbal

3. **Chunking assignments** into small, manageable tasks

4. **Nonverbal cues** to redirect behavior without shame

5. **Fidget tools** and flexible seating options

6. **Praise effort and creativity**, not just neatness or quietness

B. At Home: For Parents

1. **Designate a quiet, uncluttered homework zone**

2. **Use timers and visual schedules**

3. **Reward systems** for homework completion and effort

4. **Daily planner check-ins** with the child

5. **Avoid yelling** — use collaboration instead: "How can we solve this together?"

6. **Stay in close communication** with teachers

Section 4: IEPs, 504s, and Academic Accommodations (US Focus)

If ADHD significantly impacts learning, students may qualify for:

- **504 Plan** (civil rights-based): Provides accommodations

- **IEP** (Individualized Education Program): For those whose ADHD affects learning under IDEA law

Typical Accommodations:

- Extended time on tests

- Breaks during class or exams

- Preferential seating

- Audio versions of books

- Extra time for transitions

- Alternate testing environments

Note: Parents should request a **formal evaluation** in writing. Schools must respond by law.

Section 5: ADHD in Different Age Groups

A. Preschool–Grade 2:

- Often misdiagnosed as "just immature"
- Signs: bouncing, blurting, short attention span
- Intervention at this stage is most effective

B. Grades 3–6:

- Increased academic pressure reveals ADHD challenges
- Social rejection may begin — critical to build self-esteem
- Ideal time to introduce structure and self-talk

C. Middle School:

- Executive function demands increase
- Emotional outbursts may rise due to hormones

- Peer comparisons can hurt confidence
- Begin teaching **self-advocacy**

D. High School:

- Academic demands and poor time management may clash
- Risk of school avoidance, late work, and overwhelm
- Begin training for adult independence: planners, alarms, responsibility

E. College and Beyond:

- Legal shift: Student must advocate
- Disability office may provide accommodations
- Freedom requires new systems — time blocking, alarms, apps

Section 6: What Makes a Great Teacher for ADHD Kids

- Patience over punishment

- Humor over humiliation
- Flexibility over formality
- Belief over bias

A great teacher doesn't expect conformity. They **recognize patterns**, **adjust the system**, and **champion the child**.

Section 7: The Role of the Parent Advocate

Parents must be:

- Educated about ADHD
- Fearless in IEP/504 meetings
- Calm but assertive
- Willing to ask for outside assessments or tutors
- Ready to build their child's self-esteem every single day

Tell your child every day:
"You are not a problem. You are a person with a unique brain. And I love the way you think."

Section 8: Faith and Learning

In Jewish tradition, education is a mitzvah — a commandment. Every child is obligated to learn, and every community is obligated to teach. ADHD doesn't remove that mission — it reshapes it.

"Chanoch l'na'ar al pi darko" – *Educate a child according to their way* (Mishlei 22:6). Not *your* way. Not the system's way. **Their** way.

ADHD children may not sit still for Gemara or Math — but they may **build**, **sing**, **question**, or **lead**.

Hashem didn't make mistakes when He wired your child differently. And we shouldn't treat it like a defect. It's an invitation.

Conclusion: School Is Not the End of the Story

Many brilliant ADHD adults were told they'd never succeed in school. Many were suspended, expelled, humiliated, or silenced.

But they didn't fail. **The system failed to see them.**

Our job is not to fix the ADHD child.
It's to fix the **lens** we use to view them.

The classroom can be a prison — or a platform.
Let's build the platform.

Chapter 14: Medication, Supplements, and Natural Tools

What Helps and What Hurts

Introduction: The ADHD Toolbox Has Many Drawers

For some, medication is life-changing. For others, it's the beginning of a frustrating journey of side effects and trial-and-error. For many, the answer lies somewhere in between — a blend of pharmaceutical tools, natural supports, and daily lifestyle tweaks that unlock the best version of their brain.

This chapter offers an honest, balanced look at the tools available — not just pills, but practices — to manage ADHD with wisdom, personalization, and dignity.

Section 1: Understanding ADHD Medications

Medication is not a cure. It is a **tool** — a chemical key that can unlock clarity, focus, and calm. But it's not for everyone, and not every med works the same for every brain.

A. Stimulants

These are the most commonly prescribed medications for ADHD and include:

- **Methylphenidate-based** (Ritalin, Concerta, Focalin)
- **Amphetamine-based** (Adderall, Vyvanse, Dexedrine)

How They Work:

They increase dopamine and norepinephrine levels in the brain — chemicals that improve focus, motivation, and impulse control.

Benefits:

- Fast-acting (10–60 minutes)
- Often highly effective
- Customizable dosages

Risks and Side Effects:

- Appetite suppression

- Insomnia
- Rebound effects (crashes when it wears off)
- Tics, anxiety in some users
- Potential for abuse or misuse

B. Non-Stimulants

- **Atomoxetine (Strattera)**
- **Guanfacine (Intuniv)**
- **Clonidine (Kapvay)**
- **Bupropion (Wellbutrin)** — off-label

These are sometimes used when stimulants are not tolerated or if anxiety, tics, or sleep issues are present.

Section 2: Natural and Lifestyle-Based Supports

Medication alone is rarely enough. The ADHD brain responds powerfully to **environmental and nutritional tuning.**

A. Diet and Nutrition

1. **Protein-rich breakfast** – stabilizes blood sugar and supports neurotransmitter production

2. **Omega-3 fatty acids** – shown in studies to help with attention and mood

3. **Magnesium and Zinc** – often low in ADHD individuals; important for focus and calm

4. **Iron levels** – check ferritin; low iron linked to worsened symptoms

5. **Avoid high-sugar, high-dye processed foods** – may increase hyperactivity in sensitive individuals

B. Exercise: The Natural Ritalin

Regular movement boosts dopamine and executive function:

- 30 minutes of aerobic exercise = 2–3 hours of improved focus
- Especially helpful before school or work
- Activities like swimming, martial arts, dancing, or walking all count

C. Sleep as Medicine

ADHD disrupts sleep — and poor sleep worsens ADHD.

- Aim for consistent sleep/wake times
- Avoid screens 1 hour before bed
- Use white noise or weighted blankets
- Consider melatonin (in consultation with doctor)

Section 3: Supplements and Herbals — What the Research Shows

⚠ Always consult a medical professional before starting supplements, especially in children.

A. Omega-3 (EPA-DHA):

- Widely studied
- Improves attention and emotional regulation
- Use high-EPA formulas (1000+ mg/day)

B. Magnesium:

- Calming effect

- Helps sleep and reduces muscle tension
- 200–400 mg/day (citrate or glycinate forms)

C. Zinc:

- May improve dopamine regulation
- 20–30 mg/day (do not exceed without testing)

D. Iron:

- Only supplement if bloodwork confirms deficiency

E. L-Theanine:

- Calming amino acid from green tea
- Improves sleep and reduces anxiety

F. Rhodiola, Ginkgo Biloba, Bacopa:

- Some cognitive support shown in trials
- Use with caution — may interact with medications

Section 4: Emotional and Spiritual Tools

A. Meditation and Breathwork

Though it may seem impossible for ADHD minds, **short, structured meditation** has shown benefits:

- Guided 5–10 minute meditations
- Breath counting apps
- Body scans and muscle relaxation

Even prayer and silent reflection can function as **spiritual regulation tools**, helping the ADHD soul return to center.

B. Mindfulness Training for ADHD

Not just for calm — mindfulness trains awareness of attention itself. ADHD coaching programs now include:

- Attention awareness
- Impulse identification
- Redirection to values and goals

Section 5: Therapy and Coaching

Medication supports the chemistry. Therapy supports the **identity**.

A. CBT (Cognitive Behavioral Therapy):

- Evidence-based
- Addresses thought distortions, emotional outbursts, and self-criticism

B. ADHD Coaching:

- Focuses on strategies, accountability, goal-setting
- Can be life-changing for teens and adults

C. Family Therapy:

- Especially useful when ADHD affects home dynamics
- Helps siblings, spouses, and parents find tools — not blame

Section 6: Dangers of Overmedication and Misinformation

Some individuals are **misdiagnosed** or **overmedicated**, leading to worsening symptoms or loss of identity.

Medication should never make a person feel flat, numb, or unlike themselves. The goal is *more you*, not less.

Avoid:

- Stacking meds without monitoring
- Ignoring side effects
- Chasing academic perfection with pills
- Relying on medication while ignoring lifestyle issues

Section 7: Faith, Trust, and Healing

In Torah and other spiritual paths, healing is never one-dimensional.

Medication is not "bad" or "unholy" — it is a vessel. But **emunah (faith)** teaches that healing comes through the vessel, not from it.

Some souls need pills. Others need practices. Most need both.

ADHD is not a punishment. It is a configuration. And the tools that bring balance are gifts from above — whether they come in bottles, breath, food, or tefillah.

Conclusion: Build Your Personal Protocol

There is no one-size-fits-all.

Some will thrive on Ritalin.
Some will find healing in magnesium and movement.
Some will combine both.
Some will do neither, and still build powerful, meaningful lives.

The goal isn't to erase ADHD.
The goal is to **support it wisely, treat it holistically,** and **honor the soul within the symptoms.**

Chapter 15: Navigating Burnout, Overwhelm, and Shutdown

When the ADHD Brain Crashes and the World Keeps Spinning

Introduction: The Hidden Crash Behind the Mask

ADHD is often seen as energy, movement, and chaos — but underneath, there's another truth: **burnout**. Many people with ADHD burn bright… and then burn out. They try to keep up in a world not made for them, masking their symptoms, pushing beyond capacity — until their mind and body scream "enough."

This chapter is about recognizing, managing, and healing from those crashes — whether they look like panic, numbness, shutdown, depression, or rage.

Section 1: What Burnout Looks Like in ADHD

Unlike regular fatigue, ADHD burnout is **a full-system crash**. It's the result of living in constant tension between potential and performance, expectation and execution.

ADHD Burnout May Feel Like:

- Brain fog or "static" in your head
- Extreme emotional sensitivity or numbness
- Paralyzing procrastination — even for small tasks
- Sleep disruption
- Apathy: "I just don't care anymore"
- Avoiding people, places, or responsibilities
- Overwhelm over basic life tasks (showering, dishes, returning a text)

Section 2: Why ADHD Is Prone to Overwhelm

A. Executive Dysfunction

What looks like laziness is often paralysis — an inability to organize, sequence, and act. When simple things require enormous effort, **life becomes exhausting.**

B. Emotional Dysregulation

Minor setbacks feel massive. A forgotten email can trigger shame, panic, or meltdown. ADHDers **feel deeply** — and it drains reserves quickly.

C. Decision Fatigue

Too many choices = shutdown. ADHD brains juggle endless thoughts and options, creating constant friction.

D. Masking and Overcompensation

Years of pretending to be "normal" lead to collapse. The energy it takes to hide your symptoms is itself unsustainable.

Section 3: The Spiral of Shame and Inaction

A common ADHD loop:

1. Get overwhelmed
2. Avoid task
3. Feel guilty
4. Hate self
5. Still can't do the task

6. Spiral deeper

This is not defiance. It's distress.

The solution begins by **breaking the shame cycle**.

Section 4: First Aid for an ADHD Shutdown

When the crash happens, stop trying to "push through." Instead, use this 5-step protocol:

1. Pause the War

- Say out loud: "I am not lazy. I am overwhelmed."
- Validate your exhaustion. Don't argue with it.

2. Micro-Task Restart

- Choose the smallest possible task:
    - Brush teeth
    - Drink water
    - Text "I need help"
    - Put one sock away
- Let that be your win.

3. Regulate Your Body

- Breathe in for 4, hold for 4, out for 6
- Take a short walk
- Stretch for 30 seconds
- Eat a nourishing snack
- Hug something soft (yes, even a pillow)

4. Check the Narratives

- Ask: "What am I telling myself right now?"
- Reframe: "I am not broken. I am flooded."
- Remind: "Even small steps count."

5. Call in the Allies

- Text a trusted person: "I'm in a fog. Can you check in on me?"
- Use co-working apps, ADHD buddy systems, or accountability partners
- Ask for help without apology

Section 5: Long-Term Tools to Prevent the Burnout Cycle

A. Routines Built on Energy, Not Obligation

- Plan high-focus work during your natural brain-peak
- Allow buffer days or "low-brain" days
- Batch similar tasks (emails, errands, calls)

B. Create a Recovery Day Weekly

- No obligations
- No guilt
- Do only replenishing things (nap, nature, music, prayer, silence)

C. Say No More Often

Overwhelm often begins with **overcommitting**. Learn to say:

"I'd love to, but my plate is full."
"Not right now, but thank you for thinking of me."
"Let me check my bandwidth first."

D. Create a Shutdown Recovery Kit

- A warm drink
- Soothing playlist
- Weighted blanket
- Lavender oil
- A journal
- A list titled "Things That Help When I Forget What Helps"

Section 6: When It Looks Like Depression — But It's Not

ADHD burnout often mimics depression. But there's a key difference:

Symptom	ADHD Burnout	Clinical Depression
Mood	Fluctuates by task or environment	Persistent low mood regardless of activity
Motivation	Present but blocked	Often completely absent

Symptom	ADHD Burnout	Clinical Depression
Energy	Comes in bursts	Consistently low
Hope	"I want to do better, I just can't"	"Why bother?" or deep despair

If in doubt, seek professional support. Sometimes the two overlap, and treatment may require therapy, medication, or both.

Section 7: The Spiritual Side of Exhaustion

Even the greatest leaders in history — Moshe Rabbeinu, Eliyahu Hanavi — **crashed** from the weight of their mission.

Hashem never rebuked them. He gave them sleep, food, and kindness.

If G-d shows compassion to the burned-out, we must show it to ourselves.

There is a holiness in **rest**.
There is a mitzvah in **recovery**.

The soul was not designed to run on 100% forever. Even the sun sets to rise again.

Conclusion: Rest is Not Failure — It's Strategy

You are not lazy.
You are not broken.
You are not a disappointment.

You are tired — and you are still sacred.

ADHD burnout is not a sign you're weak.
It's a sign you've been fighting hard without the right armor.

Let this chapter be your pause.
Let tomorrow be your rebuild.

Chapter 16: Love and Marriage with ADHD

The Sacred Struggle and the Deeper Connection

Introduction: ADHD and the Challenge of Intimacy

To love with ADHD is to love fiercely — but sometimes, unevenly. It's bursts of passion followed by distraction. It's spontaneous devotion, then forgotten milk at the store. It's deep feeling, deep forgetting, deep regret, and deep longing to be better.

Marriage with ADHD is not broken love. It is *raw love* — chaotic, beautiful, unfiltered. In this chapter, we uncover the tools, truths, and spiritual insights that allow ADHD couples to not only survive — but grow stronger together.

Conclusion

As we close this journey, we reflect on the transformative power of understanding and embracing ADHD—not as a curse, but as a unique blessing. By shifting the narrative, you can discover the tremendous potential that lies within yourself or your loved ones. This is not an end, but a beginning: a path to seeing ADHD not as a barrier but as a bridge to creativity, compassion, and contribution.

ADHD: A Blessing or a Curse?
Undertone: *How to Transform the World's Most Misunderstood Brain into a Precious Gift*

Section 1: When ADHD Lives in the Marriage

ADHD affects love at every stage:

Courtship:

- Rapid bonding and excitement
- Hyperfocus on the partner
- Idealization that can fade quickly
- Deep empathy… sometimes followed by retreat

Daily Married Life:

- Missed details, late arrivals, forgotten chores
- Emotional flooding or shutdown during conflict

- Uneven workload (often with one partner "parenting" the other)
- Misunderstandings due to forgetfulness or impulsive words

Long-Term Partnership:

- Repeating cycles of guilt, apology, and self-blame
- Struggles with parenting, bills, and home systems
- But also: joy, laughter, renewal, growth — when *seen* and *worked through*

Section 2: The Emotional Landscape of an ADHD Spouse

An ADHD partner may feel:

- Constantly behind
- Unworthy of their partner's love
- Ashamed of letting them down (again)
- Explosive or avoidant when overwhelmed
- Desperate to be better, but unsure how

The non-ADHD partner may feel:

- Ignored
- Overburdened
- Resentful
- Confused by "hot and cold" emotional waves
- Like they are "alone" in the relationship

Both need to understand: these struggles are not *character flaws*. They are the dance of **two different brains** trying to find rhythm.

Section 3: Building a Loving ADHD Marriage

A. Clear, Kind Communication

- Use "I feel" statements, not accusations
- Don't assume tone — ask
- ADHD partners often don't register subtle cues — **say it directly, lovingly**

Instead of "You never listen!" try: "I feel hurt when you forget what I said. Can we try writing it down?"

B. Shared Systems Save Relationships

- Use shared digital calendars
- Whiteboards for daily tasks
- Color-coded responsibilities
- Weekly "check-in" meetings (short, focused, calm tone)
- Visual reminders for recurring items (garbage night, bills)

C. Reassign Roles by Strength, Not Tradition

Forget 50/50. ADHD marriages thrive on **custom balance**.

One partner manages paperwork. The other manages the meals. One is the dreamer. The other is the executor.

When each plays to their strength, **the team wins**.

Section 4: Rebuilding Trust After the "Same Mistake Again"

In ADHD marriages, repetition of small mistakes can feel like betrayal.

But often, they're **neurological loops**, not emotional neglect.

- Create **repair rituals**: hugs, safe apologies, short reset phrases
- **Forgive the brain** without excusing the impact
- Say: "I know you didn't mean it. Let's find a tool so it doesn't happen again."

Section 5: Intimacy and Emotional Vulnerability

ADHD and Physical Intimacy:

- Distractibility can interrupt connection
- Shame and sensory overload can block desire
- But **hyperfocus and deep empathy** can make ADHD partners attentive lovers

Emotional Vulnerability:

ADHD spouses may have trauma from years of being told they're "too much." Trust is built when their partner says:

- "You're not a project. You're a person I love."
- "You don't have to be perfect to be precious."
- "You're safe to be real with me."

Section 6: The Role of Faith and Commitment

In Torah and many spiritual traditions, **marriage is not about ease**. It's about transformation.

ADHD challenges become the *grindstone* for patience, empathy, forgiveness — and ultimately, joy.

"Ezer k'negdo" – your spouse is your help, even when they seem opposed. The friction refines the soul.

Marriage isn't just love. It's choosing again and again to **build a bayis ne'eman**, a faithful home, despite distraction, frustration, or failure.

Section 7: What a Healthy ADHD Marriage Looks Like

- They laugh, even when the keys are lost again
- They make lists, and sometimes forget the lists
- They fight fair, and return to love faster each time
- They grow because they refuse to give up
- They **love loudly**, even when life gets messy

A good ADHD marriage doesn't look like perfection. It looks like **grit, grace, and deep gratitude.**

Conclusion: Love Doesn't Need to Be Neat

Love with ADHD may never be tidy.
But it can be true.

it can be holy.
It can be healing.

If you are married to someone with ADHD, remember: you are not alone. You are dancing with a wild, beautiful storm. Learn its rhythm, protect your peace, and love its center.

If *you* are the partner with ADHD, remember:
You are worthy of love.
You are not broken.
You are becoming.

In love, the ADHD soul can find its **deepest healing** — not in being fixed, but in being fully **seen and still chosen**.

Closing Reflections: From Disorder to Design

You Were Never Broken — You Were Misunderstood

The world told you ADHD was a disorder. That you were too loud, too forgetful, too sensitive, too late, too much.

And maybe you believed it.

Maybe you spent years trying to fix yourself, blend in, shrink down, or disappear behind masks of compliance. Maybe you collapsed under the weight of everyone else's expectations — or your own impossible standards. Maybe you lost friendships. Or marriages. Or time.

But hear this now:

You are not defective.
You are not weak.
You are not beyond repair.

You are wired for **depth**, not simplicity.
For **fire**, not stillness.
For **truth**, not convenience.

ADHD is not the enemy.

Shame is.
Isolation is.
Ignorance is.

This book is not just a manual. It's a mirror.

It shows what was always true: That your brain, your journey, your storm — have meaning. That ADHD is not the full picture of who you are, but it is a powerful color in the painting.

And once you understand it, you can stop fighting it.

It's time to rewrite the story.

ADHD isn't just a label. It's a language.

A language of intensity, speed, hunger for meaning, drive for justice, flashes of genius, and moments of awe. A language that says: "There is more. I feel it. I know it. I want it. I just don't know how to get there."

Now you have the map.

To the Parent reading this:

Your child doesn't need perfection.
 They need protection.
 Protection from shame, from silence, from low expectations.
 They need you to believe in what others cannot yet see.

To the Adult with ADHD:

It's not too late.
 Not to heal. Not to grow. Not to thrive.
 You are allowed to love your mind. You are allowed to ask for help.
 You are allowed to be more than survival.

To the Teacher, the Spouse, the Employer, the Friend:

If you love someone with ADHD, **listen deeper**.
Don't just see the surface.
See the effort, the exhaustion, the heart.

You are not alone.

And you never were.

We are many. We are gifted. We are tired — but we are rising.

So take your diagnosis, your scars, your quirks, your resilience —
and **build something brilliant**.

Let ADHD be not your shame —
but your story.

And let that story be one of redemption, not regret.

The end is just the beginning.

About the Author

Rabbi Dovied Zwi van der Velde

Rabbi Dovied Zwi van der Velde was not expected to survive infancy — let alone become a rabbi, spiritual guide, life coach, builder, and voice for the misunderstood. Born after the Holocaust to parents who had lost 94% of their family, he was their miracle child — and also their deepest fear. At just two and a half years old, he was stricken with encephalitis, leaving him paralyzed and unresponsive. Doctors advised his parents to "pull the plug." But they refused. This was their only son after the war — and Hashem had given him for a reason.

A neurologist named Dr. Neo Kitchin — a Japanese physician — offered two options: the Western model of comfort with permanent disability, or the Eastern path, brutal and intense. The irony that a Japanese doctor would help save the child of a man tortured by the Japanese in the Indonesian camps was not lost on the family. But they chose the path of challenge.

His parents were instructed never to pick him up when he fell. Only to turn and encourage. Never to comfort with lies, but to build through truth. "He'll fall a hundred times," the doctor said, "but the one hundred and first time, he'll get up stronger."

And he did.

After being expelled from his first school, his grandmother, **Klara van der Velde de Vries**, placed a newspaper ad for a tutor. The response came from **Mrs. de Jong**, a 70-something Dutch woman with a mind ahead of her time and a scent of mothballs. Her tools? Sugar-laden coffee, hand-over-hand compression therapy, direct stimulation, and unwavering belief. She pulled him back each time his focus drifted. And within a year, he tested at the level of 3rd or 4th grade.

Despite this, the school board placed him in a school for difficult children. His crime? Being different. His parents, traumatized survivors, accepted it under threat that if he failed, he would be institutionalized. At the time — even in the United States — this was a common fate for children with attention issues. That school became his battlefield.

Beaten daily for being a Jew, he found his weapon in intellect. Chess became his armor. Cards became his defense. He mastered games but ignored schoolwork for nearly six years. Eventually, a teacher informed his parents that he had made no progress. His father, shocked, made a rare move: he removed him from bed during the night and brought him face to face with the man who called him a failure.

"Well," his father said, "we'll buy him a toilet brush and a coin bowl and set him up at De Beekhorve to clean toilets."

The teacher was stunned. But that moment ignited something. The next morning, Dovied requested all first-grade books. In a few months, he taught himself **six years of elementary school and two to three years of high school**. He graduated in a gray tuxedo and gave a speech that left adults breathless.

Still, the pattern repeated. He soared, then stagnated. At the prestigious **Apollo MAVO** school, the principal begged his parents to pull him out. They refused. When summoned, Dovied made a deal: "Let me change five subjects and add one more. I'll do seven instead of six." The principal laughed. But he delivered. In less than nine months, he passed all seven exams and moved forward.

Eventually, he attended college, **yeshiva in Israel, law school in Curaçao**, served as a **rabbi at age 21**, studied **electronics engineering in the U.S.**, and built a life from broken beginnings. He married, became a father and grandfather, a business owner, and a guide to others who felt out of place in a world that rewards conformity.

And yet, it wasn't until his late twenties that he even heard of ADHD. His then-wife, Chanie (Ann Sylvia Root), tried to explain what it meant. At first, he brushed it off — "just another label." But when she read him a list of successful ADHD figures, he recognized himself. Finally, his mind had a name — and a map.

He tried medications: Ritalin, Cylert, others. Most failed. They slowed him, but they didn't help him steer. What worked was mindset. Ownership. Structure. Support. He began therapy with **Dr. Abe Siegelman**, remapping his mind, retraining his executive function, and taking responsibility not only for his potential — but for his punctuality, empathy, and integrity.

Today, **Rabbi Dovied Zwi van der Velde** is a respected **realtor. rabbi, life coach, insurance professional, community leader, father of five, grandfather of twelve**, and a living testament that ADHD is not a deficit — it is a different language of brilliance.

He is the founder of *Home Safe Home Inc.*, a charitable nonprofit that turns real estate donations into housing and hope for veterans and elderly individuals who have lost everything. He is also the mind behind the *Amazing People Project*, a visionary matchmaking and support system for those with special needs.

If this book has spoken to your soul, or you see yourself or your child in its pages, please reach out.
Rabbi Dovied Zwi van der Velde

homesafehome613@gmail.com

+1 (917) 681-5189

"If I had been normal, I never would have become me."

www.ingramcontent.com/pod-product-compliance
Lightning Source LLC
Chambersburg PA
CBHW030447100526
44580CB00001B/15